THE MYSTICAL TEACHINGS OF JESUS

compiled by

David Hoffmeister

The Mystical Teachings of Jesus
Compiled by David Hoffmeister
ISBN: 978-1-942253-23-5

First Printed Edition 2016

Living Miracles Publications
P.O. Box 789, Kamas, UT 84036 USA
publishing@livingmiraclescenter.org
+1 435.200.4076

LIVING MIRACLES

This book was joyfully produced by the Living Miracles Community—a non-profit ministry run by inspired modern-day mystics devoted to awakening.

Behold, the kingdom of God is within you.

Editor's notes

- In *A Course in Miracles* the word "ego" is used synonymously with the Bible's "satan."
- Bible quotes are indented and *A Course in Miracles* quotes are not.

Bibliography

The Bible, King James Version

A Course in Miracles quotes are referenced by the following system:
T: Text
W: Workbook for Students
M: Manual for Teachers
C: Clarification of Terms
P: Psychotherapy Pamphlet
S: Song of Prayer
W-Ep: Workbook Epilogue

Example:
"All real pleasure comes from doing God's Will." (T-1.VII.1:4)
T-1.VII.1:4 = Text, Chapter 1, Section VII, Paragraph 1, Sentence 4

Welcome

The Mystical Teachings of Jesus answers the prayer of the heart for an intimate and profound relationship with God in modern times. It is for anyone who is inspired by the life and teachings of Jesus and has experienced the deep wisdom of the Bible.

The Mystical Teachings of Jesus will illuminate the mind with a deeper understanding of the teachings of the Bible and *A Course in Miracles* (ACIM). The chapters in this book contain Bible verses, side-by-side with ACIM quotes, providing a dialogue of clarity, and directly answering questions from the heart, such as: "Jesus, what is my relationship to you? What is a miracle?" and, "How will the world end?"

Two thousand years ago Jesus spoke profound words to lead us out of the darkness and into the Light and Love of His Grace. Today through *A Course in Miracles* he continues to bless the world with clear and direct teachings on forgiveness and salvation.

This book is a gateway to the deep Self Realization that we are the Christ Mind—we are love itself.

As the Bible so clearly states: "Let this mind be in you, which was also in Christ Jesus." (Philippians 2:5)

And from *A Course in Miracles*: "This is the invitation to the Holy Spirit. I have said already that I can reach up and bring the Holy Spirit down to you, but I can bring Him to you only at your own invitation. The Holy Spirit is in your right mind, as He was in Mine. The Bible says, 'May the mind be in you that was also in Christ Jesus,' and uses this as a blessing. It is the blessing of miracle-mindedness. It asks that you may think as I thought, joining with me in Christ thinking." (T-5.I.3:1-6)

David Hoffmeister was raised in a Christian family, and always felt a deep love for Jesus; ultimately he devoted himself to a complete immersion of Jesus's teachings in *A Course in Miracles*. He has become a living demonstration of one who has paid heed to these teachings and lives his life from a state of mind that is consistently loving, peaceful, and joyful! His life's purpose is to extend the message of peace.

"Seek ye first the Kingdom of Heaven and His righteousness and all else shall be added unto you." (Matthew 6:33)

"I will come in response to a single unequivocal call." (T-4.III.7:10)

*May this book comfort and bless us
on our journey Home to God.*

Contents

Who Is Jesus Christ?

> "When Jesus came into the coasts of Caesarea Philippi, he asked his disciples, saying, Whom do men say that I the Son of man am? And they said, Some say that thou art John the Baptist: some, Elias; and others, Jeremias, or one of the prophets. He saith unto them, But whom say ye that I am? And Simon Peter answered and said, Thou art the Christ, the Son of the living God." (Matthew 16:13-16)

The name of *Jesus* is the name of one who was a man but saw the face of Christ in all his brothers and remembered God. So he became identified with *Christ*, a man no longer, but at one with God. The man was an illusion, for he seemed to be a separate being, walking by himself, within a body that appeared to hold his self from Self, as all illusions do. Yet who can save unless he sees illusions and then identifies them as what they are? Jesus remains a Savior because he saw the false without accepting it as true. And Christ needed his form that He might appear to men and save them from their own illusions. (C-5.2:1-6)

In his complete identification with the Christ—the perfect Son of God, His one creation and His happiness, forever like Himself and One with Him—Jesus became what all of you must be. He led the way for you to follow him. He leads you back to God because he saw the road before him, and he followed it. ... He offered you a final demonstration that it is impossible to kill God's Son; nor can his life in any way be changed by sin and evil, malice, fear or death. (C-5.3:1-5)

And therefore all your sins have been forgiven because they carried no effects at all. And so they were but dreams. Arise with him who showed you this because you owe him this who shared your dreams that they might be dispelled. And shares them still, to be at one with you. (C-5.4:1-4)

His little life on earth was not enough to teach the mighty lesson that he learned for all of you. He will remain with you to lead you from the hell you made to God. And when you join your will with his, your sight will be his vision, for the eyes of Christ are shared. Walking with him is just as natural as walking with a brother whom you knew since you were born, for such indeed he is. ... For he will set your mind at rest at last and carry it with you unto your God. (C-5.5:3-9)

"Enter in at the strait gate: for wide is the gate, and broad is the way, that leadeth to destruction, and many there be which go in thereat: Because strait is the gate, and narrow is the way, which leadeth unto life, and few there be that find it." (Matthew 7:13-14)

"So the last shall be first, and the first last: for many be called, but few chosen." (Matthew 20:16)

"Take my yoke upon you, and learn of me; for I am meek and lowly in heart: and ye shall find rest unto your souls." (Matthew 11:29)

I was a man who remembered spirit and its knowledge. As a man I did not attempt to counteract error with knowledge, but to correct error from the bottom up. I demonstrated both the powerlessness of the body and the power of the mind. By uniting my will with that of my Creator, I naturally remembered spirit and its real purpose. I cannot unite your will with God's for you, but I can erase all misperceptions from your mind if you will bring it under my guidance. Only your misperceptions stand in your way. Without them your choice is certain. Sane perception induces sane choosing. I cannot choose for you, but I can help you make your own right choice. (T-3.IV.7:3-11)

"Then saith he unto his disciples, The harvest truly is plenteous, but the labourers are few. Pray ye therefore the Lord of the harvest, that he will send forth labourers into his harvest." (Matthew 9:37-38)

"And he began to speak unto them by parables. A man planted a vineyard, and set an hedge about it, and digged a place for the winefat, and built a tower, and let it out to husbandmen, and went into a far country. And at the season he sent to the husbandmen a servant, that he might receive from the husbandmen of the fruit of the vineyard. And they caught him, and beat him, and sent him away empty.

And again he sent unto them another servant; and at him they cast stones, and wounded him in the head, and sent him away shamefully handled. And again he sent another; and him they killed, and many others; beating some, and killing some. Having yet therefore one son, his wellbeloved, he sent him also last unto them, saying, They will reverence my son.

But those husbandmen said among themselves, This is the heir; come, let us kill him, and the inheritance shall be ours. And they took him, and killed him, and cast him out of the vineyard." (Mark 12:1-8)

"If the world hate you, ye know that it hated me before it hated you. If ye were of the world, the world would love his own: but because ye are not of the world, but I have chosen you out of the world, therefore the world hateth you. Remember the word that I said unto you, The servant is not greater than his lord. If they have persecuted me, they will also persecute you; if they have kept my saying, they will keep yours also. But all these things will they do unto you for my name's sake, because they know not him that sent me. If I had not come and spoken unto them, they had not had sin: but now they have no cloak for their sin. He that hateth me hateth my Father also. If I had not done among them the works which none other man did, they had not had sin: but now have they both seen and hated both me and my Father. But this cometh to pass, that the word might be fulfilled that is written in their law, They hated me without a cause." (John 15:18-25)

My mission was simply to unite the will of the Sonship with the Will of the Father by being aware of the Father's Will myself. This is the awareness I came to give you, and your problem in accepting it is the problem of this world. ... The world must therefore despise and reject me, because the world *is* the belief that love is impossible. (T-8.IV.3:4-7)

"The next day John seeth Jesus coming unto him, and saith, Behold the Lamb of God, which taketh away the sin of the world." (John 1:29)

"The wolf also shall dwell with the lamb, and the leopard shall lie down with the kid; and the calf and the young lion and the fatling together; and a little child shall lead them." (Isaiah 11:6)

"Blessed are the pure in heart: for they shall see God." (Matthew 5:8)

I have been correctly referred to as "the lamb of God who taketh away the sins of the world," but those who represent the lamb as blood-stained do not understand the meaning of the symbol. Correctly understood, it is a very simple symbol that speaks of my innocence. The lion and the lamb lying down together symbolize that strength and innocence are not in conflict, but naturally live in peace. "Blessed are the pure in heart for they shall see God" is another way of saying the same thing. A pure mind knows the truth and this is its strength. It does not confuse destruction with innocence because it associates innocence with strength, not with weakness. (T-3.I.5:1-6)

> "These things I have spoken unto you, that in me ye might have peace. In the world ye shall have tribulation: but be of good cheer; I have overcome the world." (John 16:33)

> "He that overcometh shall inherit all things; and I will be his God, and he shall be my son." (Revelation 21:7)

My purpose, then, is still to overcome the world. I do not attack it, but my light must dispel it because of what it is. Light does not attack darkness, but it does shine it away. (T-8.IV.2:8-10)

But if I surmounted guilt and overcame the world, you were with me. Would you see in me the symbol of guilt or of the end of guilt, remembering that what I signify to you you see within yourself? (T-19.IV.B.6:5-6)

> "Jesus said unto them, Verily, verily, I say unto you, Before Abraham was, I am." (John 8:58)

> "I am Alpha and Omega, the beginning and the end." (Revelations 21:6)

Right perception is necessary before God can communicate directly to His altars, which He established in His Sons. There He can communicate His certainty, and His knowledge will bring peace without question. God is not a stranger to His Sons, and His Sons are not strangers to each other. Knowledge preceded both perception and time, and will ultimately replace them. That is the real meaning of "Alpha and Omega, the beginning and the end," and "Before Abraham was I am." Perception can and must be stabilized, but knowledge *is* stable. (T-3.III.6:1-6)

Jesus, What Is My Relationship to You?

> "I am the vine, ye are the branches: He that abideth in me, and I in him, the same bringeth forth much fruit: for without me ye can do nothing." (John 15:5)

> "For whom he did foreknow, he also did predestinate to be conformed to the image of his Son, that he might be the firstborn among many brethren." (Romans 8:29)

> "Be ye therefore perfect, even as your Father which is in heaven is perfect." (Matthew 5:48)

You are a perfect creation, and should experience awe only in the Presence of the Creator of perfection. The miracle is therefore a sign of love among equals. Equals should not be in awe of one another because awe implies inequality. It is therefore an inappropriate reaction to me. An elder brother is entitled to respect for his greater experience, and obedience for his greater wisdom. He is also entitled to love because he is a brother, and to devotion if he is devoted. It is only my devotion that entitles me to yours. There is nothing about me that you cannot attain. I have nothing that does not come from God. The difference between us now is that I have nothing else. This leaves me in a state which is only potential in you. (T-1.II.3:3-13)

> "As a man thinketh in his heart, so is he." (Proverbs 23:7)

You are the work of God, and His work is wholly lovable and wholly loving. This is how a man must think of himself in his heart, because this is what he is. (T-1.III.2:3-4)

> "Jesus saith unto him, I am the way, the truth, and the life: no man cometh unto the Father, but by me." (John 14:6)

> "I and my Father are one." (John 10:30)

> "Ye have heard how I said unto you, I go away, and come again unto you. If ye loved me, ye would rejoice, because I said, I go unto the Father: for my Father is greater than I." (John 14:28)

"No man cometh unto the Father but by me" does not mean that I am in any way separate or different from you except in time, and time does not really exist. The statement is more meaningful in terms of a vertical rather than a horizontal axis. You stand below me and I stand below God. In the process of "rising up," I am higher because without me the distance between God and man would be too great for you to encompass. I bridge the distance as an elder brother to you on the one hand, and as a Son of God on the other. My devotion to my brothers has placed me in charge of the Sonship, which I render complete because I share it. This may appear to contradict the statement "I and my Father are one," but there are two parts to the statement in recognition that the Father is greater. (T-1.II.4:1-7)

We are still equal as learners, although we do not need to have equal experiences. The Holy Spirit is glad when you can learn from mine, and be reawakened by them. That is their only purpose, and that is the only way in which I can be perceived as the way, the truth and the life. (T-6.I.10:1-3)

> "Jesus said unto her, I am the resurrection, and the life: he that believeth in me, though he were dead, yet shall he live. And whosoever liveth and believeth in me shall never die." (John 11:25-26)

I am *your* resurrection and *your* life. You live in me because you live in God. And everyone lives in you, as you live in everyone. Can you, then, perceive unworthiness in a brother and not perceive it in yourself? And can you perceive it in yourself and not perceive it in God? Believe in the resurrection because it has been accomplished, and it has been accomplished in you. This is as true now as it will ever be, for the resurrection is the Will of God, which knows no time and no exceptions. But make no exceptions yourself, or you will not perceive what has been accomplished for you. For we ascend unto the Father together, as it was in the beginning, is now and ever shall be, for such is the nature of God's Son as his Father created him. (T-11.VI.4:1-9)

The miracle of life is ageless, born in time but nourished in eternity. (T-19.IV.C.10:6)

> "Heaven and earth shall pass away, but my words shall not pass away." (Matthew 24:35)

"Heaven and earth shall pass away" means that they will not continue to exist as separate states. My word, which is the resurrection and the life, shall not pass away because life is eternal. (T-1.III.2:1-2)

Speak on the Parable of the Prodigal Son

"And he said, A certain man had two sons:

And the younger of them said to his father, Father, give me the portion of goods that falleth to me. And he divided unto them his living.

And not many days after the younger son gathered all together, and took his journey into a far country, and there wasted his substance with riotous living. And when he had spent all, there arose a mighty famine in that land; and he began to be in want. And he went and joined himself to a citizen of that country; and he sent him into his fields to feed swine.

And he would fain have filled his belly with the husks that the swine did eat: and no man gave unto him. And when he came to himself, he said, How many hired servants of my father's have bread enough and to spare, and I perish with hunger!

I will arise and go to my father, and will say unto him, Father, I have sinned against heaven, and before thee, And am no more worthy to be called thy son: make me as one of thy hired servants. And he arose, and came to his father. But when he was yet a great way off, his father saw him, and had compassion, and ran, and fell on his neck, and kissed him.

And the son said unto him, Father, I have sinned against heaven, and in thy sight, and am no more worthy to be called thy son.

But the father said to his servants, Bring forth the best robe, and put it on him; and put a ring on his hand, and shoes on his feet:

And bring hither the fatted calf, and kill it; and let us eat, and be merry: For this my son was dead, and is alive again; he was lost, and is found. And they began to be merry.

> Now his elder son was in the field: and as he came and drew nigh to the house, he heard music and dancing. And he called one of the servants, and asked what these things meant. And he said unto him, Thy brother is come; and thy father hath killed the fatted calf, because he hath received him safe and sound. And he was angry, and would not go in: therefore came his father out, and entreated him. And he answering said to his father, Lo, these many years do I serve thee, neither transgressed I at any time thy commandment: and yet thou never gavest me a kid, that I might make merry with my friends: But as soon as this thy son was come, which hath devoured thy living with harlots, thou hast killed for him the fatted calf.
>
> And he said unto him, Son, thou art ever with me, and all that I have is thine.
>
> It was meet that we should make merry, and be glad: for this thy brother was dead, and is alive again; and was lost, and is found." (Luke 15:11-32)

Listen to the story of the prodigal son, and learn what God's treasure is and yours: This son of a loving father left his home and thought he had squandered everything for nothing of any value, although he had not understood its worthlessness at the time. He was ashamed to return to his father, because he thought he had hurt him. Yet when he came home the father welcomed him with joy, because the son himself *was* his father's treasure. He wanted nothing else. (T-8.VI.4:1-4)

What God has willed for you *is* yours. He has given His Will to His treasure, whose treasure it is. Your heart lies where your treasure is, as His does. You who are beloved of God are wholly blessed. Learn this of me, and free the holy will of all those who are as blessed as you are. (T-8.VI.10:1-5)

All your striving must be directed against littleness, for it does require vigilance to protect your magnitude in this world. To hold your magnitude in perfect awareness in a world of littleness is a task the little cannot undertake. Yet it is asked of you, in tribute to your magnitude and not your littleness. Nor is it asked of you alone. The power of God will support every effort you make on behalf of His dear Son. Search for the little, and you deny yourself His power. God is not willing that His Son be content with less than everything. For He is not content without His Son, and His Son cannot be content with less than his Father has given him. (T-15.III.4:4-11)

> "And His name shall be called Wonderful, Counsellor, The mighty God, The everlasting Father, The Prince of Peace." (Isaiah 9:6)

> "Another parable put he forth unto them, saying, The kingdom of heaven is like to a grain of mustard seed, which a man took, and sowed in his field: Which indeed is the least of all seeds: but when it is grown, it is the greatest among herbs, and becometh a tree, so that the birds of the air come and lodge in the branches thereof." (Matthew 13:31-32)

Is it a sacrifice to leave littleness behind, and wander not in vain? It is not sacrifice to wake to glory. But it is sacrifice to accept anything less than glory. Learn that you must be worthy of the Prince of Peace, born in you in honor of Him Whose host you are. You know not what love means because you have sought to purchase it with little gifts, thus valuing it too little to understand its magnitude. Love is not little and love dwells in you, for you are host to Him. Before the greatness that lives in you, your poor appreciation of yourself and all the little offerings you give slip into nothingness. (T-15.III.8:1-7)

Speak on the Creation and the Fall of Man

> "All things were made by him; and without him was not any thing made that was made." (John 1:3)

Everything meets in God, because everything was created by Him and in Him. (T-6.II.7:6)

God created His Sons by extending His Thought, and retaining the extensions of His Thought in His Mind. All His Thoughts are thus perfectly united within themselves and with each other. The Holy Spirit enables you to perceive this wholeness *now.* God created you to create. You cannot extend His Kingdom until you know of its wholeness. (T-6.II.8:1-5)

He is the Prime Creator, because He created His co-creators. Because He did, time applies neither to Him nor to what He created. (T-7.I.7:6-7)

> "And God said, Let there be light: and there was light." (Genesis 1:3)

When God said, "Let there be light," there *was* light. (T-9.V.6:2)

The undivided will of the Sonship is the perfect creator, being wholly in the likeness of God, Whose Will it is. You cannot be exempt from it if you are to understand what it is and what you are. (T-8.V.2:1-2)

> "And God said, Let us make man in our image, after our likeness." (Genesis 1:26)

The statement "God created man in his own image and likeness" needs reinterpretation. "Image" can be understood as "thought," and "likeness" as "of a like quality." God did create spirit in His Own Thought and of a quality like to His Own. There *is* nothing else. (T-3.V.7:1-4)

To extend is a fundamental aspect of God which He gave to His Son. In the creation, God extended Himself to His creations and imbued them with the same loving Will to create. You have not only been fully created, but have also been created perfect. There is no emptiness in you. Because of your likeness to your Creator you are creative. No child of God can lose this ability because it is inherent in what he is, but he can use it inappropriately by projecting. The inappropriate use of extension, or projection, occurs when you believe that some emptiness or lack exists in you, and that you can fill it with your own ideas instead of truth. (T-2.I.1:1-7)

While lack does not exist in the creation of God, it is very apparent in what you have made. It is, in fact, the essential difference between them. Lack implies that you would be better off in a state somehow different from the one you are in. Until the "separation," which is the meaning of the "fall," nothing was lacking. There were no needs at all. Needs arise only when you deprive yourself. You act according to the particular order of needs you establish. This, in turn, depends on your perception of what you are. (T-1.VI.1:3-10)

> "And the LORD God commanded the man, saying, Of every tree of the garden thou mayest freely eat:
>
> But of the tree of the knowledge of good and evil, thou shalt not eat of it: for in the day that thou eatest thereof thou shalt surely die." (Genesis 2:16-17)
>
> "And when the woman saw that the tree was good for food, and that it was pleasant to the eyes, and a tree to be desired to make one wise, she took of the fruit thereof, and did eat, and gave also unto her husband with her; and he did eat.
>
> And the eyes of them both were opened, and they knew that they were naked; and they sewed fig leaves together, and made themselves aprons.
>
> And they heard the voice of the LORD God walking in the garden in the cool of the day: and Adam and his wife hid themselves from the presence of the LORD God amongst the trees of the garden." (Genesis 3:6-8)

The separation is a system of thought real enough in time, though not in eternity. All beliefs are real to the believer. The fruit of only one tree was "forbidden" in the symbolic garden. But God could not have forbidden it, or it could not have *been* eaten. If God knows His children, and I assure you that He does, would He have put them in a position where their own destruction was possible? The "forbidden tree" was named the "tree of knowledge." Yet God created knowledge and gave it freely to His creations. The symbolism here has been given many interpretations, but you may be sure that any interpretation that sees either God or His creations as capable of destroying Their Own purpose is in error. (T-3.VII.3:2-9)

The Garden of Eden, or the pre-separation condition, was a state of mind in which nothing was needed. When Adam listened to the "lies of the serpent," all he heard was untruth. You do not have to continue to believe what is not true unless you choose to do so. All that can literally disappear in the twinkling of an eye because it is merely a misperception. What is seen in dreams seems to be very real. Yet the Bible says that a deep sleep fell upon Adam, and nowhere is there reference to his waking up. The world has not yet experienced any comprehensive reawakening or rebirth. Such a rebirth is impossible as long as you continue to project or miscreate. It still remains within you, however, to extend as God extended His Spirit to you. In reality this is your only choice, because your free will was given you for your joy in creating the perfect. (T-2.I.3:1-10)

God does not believe in retribution. His Mind does not create that way. He does not hold your "evil" deeds against you. Is it likely that He would hold them against me? Be very sure that you recognize how utterly impossible this assumption is, and how entirely it arises from projection. This kind of error is responsible for a host of related errors, including the belief that God rejected Adam and forced him out of the Garden of Eden. (T-3.I.3:4-9)

> "And they shall teach my people the difference between the holy and profane, and cause them to discern between the unclean and the clean." (Ezekiel 44:23)
>
> "Another parable put he forth unto them, saying, The kingdom of heaven is likened unto a man which sowed good seed in his field: But while men slept, his enemy came and sowed tares among the wheat, and went his way. But when the blade was sprung up, and brought forth fruit, then appeared the tares also. So the servants of the householder came and said unto him, Sir, didst not thou sow good seed in thy field? from whence then hath it tares? He said unto them, An enemy hath done this. The servants said unto him, Wilt thou then that we go and gather them up? But he said, Nay; lest while ye gather up the tares, ye root up also the wheat with them.

> Let both grow together until the harvest: and in the time of harvest I will say to the reapers, Gather ye together first the tares, and bind them in bundles to burn them: but gather the wheat into my barn." (Matthew 13:24-30)

> "And he said, So is the kingdom of God, as if a man should cast seed into the ground; And should sleep, and rise night and day, and the seed should spring and grow up, he knoweth not how. For the earth bringeth forth fruit of herself; first the blade, then the ear, after that the full corn in the ear. But when the fruit is brought forth, immediately he putteth in the sickle, because the harvest is come." (Mark 4:26-29)

> "And God saw every thing that he had made, and, behold, it was very good." (Genesis 1:31)

The first step toward freedom involves a sorting out of the false from the true. This is a process of separation in the constructive sense, and reflects the true meaning of the Apocalypse. Everyone will ultimately look upon his own creations and choose to preserve only what is good, just as God Himself looked upon what He had created and knew that it was good. At this point, the mind can begin to look with love on its own creations because of their worthiness. At the same time the mind will inevitably disown its miscreations which, without belief, will no longer exist. (T-2.VIII.4:1-5)

> "Do ye look on things after the outward appearance?" (2 Corinthians 10:7)

> "For the things which are seen are temporal; but the things which are not seen are eternal." (2 Corinthians 4:18)

What God did not create does not exist. And everything that does exist exists as He created it. (W-14.1:2-3)

Perception, on the other hand, is impossible without a belief in "more" and "less." At every level it involves selectivity. Perception is a continual process of accepting and rejecting, organizing and reorganizing, shifting and changing. Evaluation is an essential part of perception, because judgments are necessary in order to select. (T-3.V.7:5-8)

Knowledge is truth, under one law, the law of love or God. Truth is unalterable, eternal and unambiguous. It can be unrecognized, but it cannot be changed. It applies to everything that God created, and only what He created is real. ... It has no opposite; no beginning and no end. It merely is. (*A Course in Miracles* Preface)

The world of perception, on the other hand, is the world of time, of change, of beginnings and endings. It is based on interpretation, not on facts. It is the world of birth and death, founded on the belief in scarcity, loss, separation and death. It is learned rather than given, selective in its perceptual emphases, unstable in its functioning, and inaccurate in its interpretations. (*A Course in Miracles* Preface)

From knowledge and perception respectively, two distinct thought systems arise which are opposite in every respect. In the realm of knowledge no thoughts exist apart from God, because God and His Creation share one Will. The world of perception, however, is made by the belief in opposites and separate wills, in perpetual conflict with each other and with God. What perception sees and hears appears to be real because it permits into awareness only what conforms to the wishes of the perceiver. This leads to a world of illusions, a world which needs constant defense precisely *because* it is not real. (*A Course in Miracles* Preface)

When you have been caught in the world of perception you are caught in a dream. You cannot escape without help, because everything your senses show merely witnesses to the reality of the dream. God has provided the Answer, the only Way out, the true Helper. ... It is the Holy Spirit's goal to help us escape from the dream world by teaching us how to reverse our thinking and unlearn our mistakes. Forgiveness is the Holy Spirit's great learning aid in bringing this thought reversal about. (*A Course in Miracles* Preface)

> "Then said his wife unto him, Dost thou still retain thine integrity? Curse God, and die." (Job 2:9)

The special ones are all asleep, surrounded by a world of loveliness they do not see. Freedom and peace and joy stand there, beside the bier on which they sleep, and call them to come forth and waken from their dream of death. Yet they hear nothing. They are lost in dreams of specialness. They hate the call that would awaken them, and they curse God because He did not make their dream reality. Curse God and die, but not by Him Who made not death; but only in the dream. Open your eyes a little; see the savior God gave to you that you might look on him, and give him back his birthright. It is yours. (T-24.III.7:1-8)

> "There is nothing covered, that shall not be revealed; and hid, that shall not be known." (Matthew 10:26)

> "And ye shall know the truth, and the truth shall make you free." (John 8:32)

You who have tried to banish love have not succeeded, but you who choose to banish fear must succeed. The Lord is with you, but you know it not. Yet your Redeemer liveth, and abideth in you in the peace out of which He was created. Would you not exchange this awareness for the awareness of fear? When we have overcome fear—not by hiding it, not by minimizing it, and not by denying its full import in any way—this is what you will really see. You cannot lay aside the obstacles to real vision without looking upon them, for to lay aside means to judge against. If you will look, the Holy Spirit will judge, and He will judge truly. Yet He cannot shine away what you keep hidden, for you have not offered it to Him and He cannot take it from you. (T-12.II.9:1-8)

All fear is ultimately reducible to the basic misperception that you have the ability to usurp the power of God. Of course, you neither can nor have been able to do this. Here is the real basis for your escape from fear. The escape is brought about by your acceptance of the Atonement, which enables you to realize that your errors never really occurred. Only after the deep sleep fell upon Adam could he experience nightmares. If a light is suddenly turned on while someone is dreaming a fearful dream, he may initially interpret the light itself as part of his dream and be afraid of it. However, when he awakens, the light is correctly perceived as the release from the dream, which is then no longer accorded reality. This release does not depend on illusions. The knowledge that illuminates not only sets you free, but also shows you clearly that you *are* free. (T-2.I.4:1-9)

Knowing is not open to interpretation. You may try to "interpret" meaning, but this is always open to error because it refers to the *perception* of meaning. (T-3.V.5:1-2)

How Is Fear Abolished?

> "There is no fear in love; but perfect love casteth out fear: because fear hath torment. He that feareth is not made perfect in love." (1 John 4:18)

> "For by grace are ye saved through faith; and that not of yourselves: it is the gift of God." (Ephesians 2:8)

Perfect love casts out fear.
If fear exists,
Then there is not perfect love.
But:
Only perfect love exists.
If there is fear,
It produces a state that does not exist.

Believe this and you will be free. Only God can establish this solution, and this faith *is* His gift. (T-1.VI.5:4-10)

There is no fear in perfect love. We will but be making perfect to you what is already perfect in you. You do not fear the unknown but the known. You will not fail in your mission because I did not fail in mine. (T-12.II.8:1-4)

> "This then is the message which we have heard of him, and declare unto you, that God is light, and in him is no darkness at all." (1 John 1:5)

The joy of learning that darkness has no power over the Son of God is the happy lesson the Holy Spirit teaches, and would have you teach with Him. (T-14.III.6:6)

Nothing and everything cannot coexist. To believe in one is to deny the other. Fear is really nothing and love is everything. Whenever light enters darkness, the darkness is abolished. ... It should be emphasized, however, that ultimately no compromise is possible between everything and nothing. Time is essentially a device by which all compromise in this respect can be given up. It only seems to be abolished by degrees, because time itself involves intervals that do not exist. Miscreation made this necessary as a corrective device. (T-2.VII.5:1-13)

> "Verily I say unto you, Except ye be converted, and become as little children, ye shall not enter into the kingdom of heaven. Whosoever therefore shall humble himself as this little child, the same is greatest in the kingdom of heaven." (Matthew 18:3-4)

"Except ye become as little children" means that unless you fully recognize your complete dependence on God, you cannot know the real power of the Son in his true relationship with the Father. (T-1.V.3:4)

The Bible tells you to become as little children. Little children recognize that they do not understand what they perceive, and so they ask what it means. Do not make the mistake of believing that you understand what you perceive, for its meaning is lost to you. Yet the Holy Spirit has saved its meaning for you, and if you will let Him interpret it, He will restore to you what you have thrown away. Yet while you think you know its meaning, you will see no need to ask it of Him. (T-11.VIII.2:1-5)

Is Distorted Perception— Lack of Vision—the Main Problem?

> "Where there is no vision, the people perish: but he that keepeth the law, happy is he." (Proverbs 29:18)

> "When I was a child, I spake as a child, I understood as a child, I thought as a child: but when I became a man, I put away childish things. For now we see through a glass, darkly; but then face to face: now I know in part; but then shall I know even as also I am known." (1 Corinthians 13:11-12)

Your mind is filled with schemes to save the face of your ego, and you do not seek the face of Christ. The glass in which the ego seeks to see its face is dark indeed. How can it maintain the trick of its existence except with mirrors? But where you look to find yourself is up to you. (T-4.IV.1:5-8)

I have said that you cannot change your mind by changing your behavior, but I have also said, and many times, that you *can* change your mind. When your mood tells you that you have chosen wrongly, and this is so whenever you are not joyous, then *know this need not be.* In every case you have thought wrongly about some brother God created, and are perceiving images your ego makes in a darkened glass. Think honestly what you have thought that God would not have thought, and what you have not thought that God would have you think. Search sincerely for what you have done and left undone accordingly, and then change your mind to think with God's. This may seem hard to do, but it is much easier than trying to think against it. Your mind is one with God's. Denying this and thinking otherwise has held your ego together, but has literally split your mind. As a loving brother I am deeply concerned with your mind, and urge you to follow my example as you look at yourself and at your brother, and see in both the glorious creations of a glorious Father. (T-4.IV.2:1-9)

> "The LORD make his face shine upon thee, and be gracious unto thee: The LORD lift up his countenance upon thee, and give thee peace." (Numbers 6:25-26)

You are a mirror of truth, in which God Himself shines in perfect light. To the ego's dark glass you need but say, "I will not look there because I know these images are not true." Then let the Holy One shine on you in peace, knowing that this and only this must be. His Mind shone on you in your creation and brought your mind into being. His Mind still shines on you and must shine through you. Your ego cannot prevent Him from shining on you, but it can prevent you from letting Him shine through you. (T-4.IV.9:1-6)

When I said "I am come as a light into the world," I meant that I came to share the light with you. Remember my reference to the ego's dark glass, and remember also that I said, "Do not look there." It is still true that where you look to find yourself is up to you. (T-5.VI.11:1-3)

> "And he said, Go, and tell this people, Hear ye indeed, but understand not; and see ye indeed, but perceive not. Make the heart of this people fat, and make their ears heavy, and shut their eyes; lest they see with their eyes, and hear with their ears, and understand with their heart, and convert, and be healed." (Isaiah 6:9-10)

> "For since the beginning of the world men have not heard, nor perceived by the ear, neither hath the eye seen, O God, beside thee, what he hath prepared for him that waiteth for him." (Isaiah 64:4)

> "Therefore speak I to them in parables: because they seeing see not; and hearing they hear not, neither do they understand." (Matthew 13:13)

> "For, behold, I create new heavens and a new earth: and the former shall not be remembered, nor come into mind." (Isaiah 65:17)

What is one cannot be perceived as separate, and the denial of the separation is the reinstatement of knowledge. (T-12.VI.7:1)

When you made visible what is not true, what *is* true became invisible to you. Yet it cannot be invisible in itself, for the Holy Spirit sees it with perfect clarity. It is invisible to you because you are looking at something else. Yet it is no more up to you to decide what is visible and what is invisible, than it is up to you to decide what reality is. What can be seen is what the Holy Spirit sees. The definition of reality is God's, not yours. He created it, and He knows what it is. You who knew have forgotten, and unless He had given you a way to remember you would have condemned yourself to oblivion. (T-12.VIII.3:1-8)

You have been wrong about the world because you have misjudged yourself. From such a twisted reference point, what could you see? All seeing starts with the perceiver, who judges what is true and what is false. And what he judges false he does not see. You who would judge reality cannot see it, for whenever judgment enters reality has slipped away. The out of mind *is* out of sight, because what is denied is there but is not recognized. Christ is still there, although you know Him not. His Being does not depend upon your recognition. He lives within you in the quiet present, and waits for you to leave the past behind and enter into the world He holds out to you in love. (T-13.VII.5:1-9)

The separation is merely a faulty formulation of reality, with no effect at all. (T-13.VIII.3:5)

> "This is my commandment, That ye love one another, as I have loved you. Greater love hath no man than this, that a man lay down his life for his friends. Ye are my friends, if ye do whatsoever I command you. Henceforth I call you not servants; for the servant knoweth not what his lord doeth: but I have called you friends; for all things that I have heard of my Father I have made known unto you." (John 15:12-15)

> "Having eyes, see ye not? and having ears, hear ye not? and do ye not remember?" (Mark 8:18)

You look still with the body's eyes, and they can see but thorns. Yet you have asked for and received another sight. Those who accept the Holy Spirit's purpose as their own share also His vision. And what enables Him to see His purpose shine forth from every altar now is yours as well as His. He sees no strangers; only dearly loved and loving friends. He sees no thorns but only lilies, gleaming in the gentle glow of peace that shines on everything He looks upon and loves. (T-20.II.5:1-6)

Such is my will for you and your brother, and for each of you for one another and for himself. Here there is only holiness and joining without limit. For what is Heaven but union, direct and perfect, and without the veil of fear upon it? Here are we one, looking with perfect gentleness upon each other and on ourselves. Here all thoughts of any separation between us become impossible. You who were a prisoner in separation are now made free in Paradise. And here would I unite with you, my friend, my brother and my Self. (T-20.III.10:1-7)

How Does What I Perceive Relate to the Golden Rule?

> "Therefore all things whatsoever ye would that men should do to you, do ye even so to them: for this is the law of the prophets." (Matthew 7:12)

You respond to what you perceive, and as you perceive so shall you behave. The Golden Rule asks you to do unto others as you would have them do unto you. This means that the perception of both must be accurate. The Golden Rule is the rule for appropriate behavior. You cannot behave appropriately unless you perceive correctly. Since you and your neighbor are equal members of one family, as you perceive both so you will do to both. You should look out from the perception of your own holiness to the holiness of others. (T-1.III.6:1-7)

> "The soul of the wicked desireth evil: his neighbour findeth no favour in his eyes." (Proverbs 21:10)

> "And why beholdest thou the mote that is in thy brother's eye, but considerest not the beam that is in thine own eye? Or how wilt thou say to thy brother, Let me pull out the mote out of thine eye; and, behold, a beam is in thine own eye? Thou hypocrite, first cast out the beam out of thine own eye; and then shalt thou see clearly to cast out the mote out of thy brother's eye." (Matthew 7:3-5)

If you perceive offense in a brother pluck the offense from your mind, for you are offended by Christ and are deceived in Him. Heal in Christ and be not offended by Him, for there is no offense in Him. If what you perceive offends you, you are offended in yourself and are condemning God's Son whom God condemneth not. Let the Holy Spirit remove all offenses of God's Son against himself and perceive no one but through His guidance, for He would save you from all condemnation. Accept His healing power and use it for all He sends you, for He wills to heal the Son of God, in whom He is not deceived. (T-11.VIII.12:1-5)

Release from guilt as you would be released. There is no other way to look within and see the light of love, shining as steadily and as surely as God Himself has always loved His Son. *And as His Son loves Him.* (T-13.X.10:1-3)

To witness sin and yet forgive it is a paradox that reason cannot see. For it maintains what has been done to you deserves no pardon. And by giving it, you grant your brother mercy but retain the proof he is not really innocent. The sick remain accusers. They cannot forgive their brothers and themselves as well. For no one in whom true forgiveness rests can suffer. He holds not the proof of sin before his brother's eyes. And thus he must have overlooked it and removed it from his own. (T-27.II.3:1-8)

> "But their minds were blinded: for until this day remaineth the same vail untaken away in the reading of the old testament; which vail is done away in Christ." (2 Corinthians 3:14)

> "And I will give unto thee the keys of the kingdom of heaven: and whatsoever thou shalt bind on earth shall be bound in heaven: and whatsoever thou shalt loose on earth shall be loosed in heaven." (Matthew 16:19)

You do not believe the Son of God is guiltless because you see the past, and see him not. When you condemn a brother you are saying, "I who was guilty choose to remain so." You have denied his freedom, and by so doing you have denied the witness unto yours. You could as easily have freed him from the past, and lifted from his mind the cloud of guilt that binds him to it. And in his freedom would have been your own. (T-13.IX.4:3-7)

Therefore, hold no one prisoner. Release instead of bind, for thus are you made free. The way is simple. (W-192.9:1-3)

What Is a Miracle?

> "Thou shalt not avenge, nor bear any grudge against the children of thy people, but thou shalt love thy neighbour as thyself." (Leviticus 19:18)

A miracle is a service. ... It is a way of loving your neighbor as yourself. You recognize your own and your neighbor's worth simultaneously. (T-1.I.18:1-4)

Miracles are teaching devices for demonstrating it is as blessed to give as to receive. They simultaneously increase the strength of the giver and supply strength to the receiver. (T-1.I.16:1-2)

> "A certain man went down from Jerusalem to Jericho, and fell among thieves, which stripped him of his raiment, and wounded him, and departed, leaving him half dead. And by chance there came down a certain priest that way: and when he saw him, he passed by on the other side. And likewise a Levite, when he was at the place, came and looked on him, and passed by on the other side.
>
> But a certain Samaritan, as he journeyed, came where he was: and when he saw him, he had compassion on him, And went to him, and bound up his wounds, pouring in oil and wine, and set him on his own beast, and brought him to an inn, and took care of him. And on the morrow when he departed, he took out two pence, and gave them to the host, and said unto him, Take care of him; and whatsoever thou spendest more, when I come again, I will repay thee. Which now of these three, thinkest thou, was neighbour unto him that fell among the thieves? And he said, He that showed mercy on him. Then said Jesus unto him, Go, and do thou likewise." (Luke 10:30-37)

> "Verily I say unto you, Inasmuch as ye have done unto one of the least of these my brethren, ye have done unto me." (Matthew 25:40)

When you offer a miracle to any of my brothers, you do it to *yourself* and me. ... When you have been restored to the recognition of your original state, you naturally become part of the Atonement yourself. As you share my unwillingness to accept error in yourself and others, you must join the great crusade to correct it; listen to my voice, learn to undo error and act to correct it. The power to work miracles belongs to you. I will provide the opportunities to do them, but you must be ready and willing. Doing them will bring conviction in the ability, because conviction comes through accomplishment. The ability is the potential, the achievement is its expression, and the Atonement, which is the natural profession of the children of God, is the purpose. (T-1.III.1:2-10)

> "Give, and it shall be given unto you; good measure, pressed down, and shaken together, and running over, shall men give into your bosom. For with the same measure that ye mete withal it shall be measured to you again." (Luke 6:38)

By giving you receive. But to receive is to accept, not to get. It is impossible not to have, but it is possible not to know you have. The recognition of having is the willingness for giving, and only by this willingness can you recognize what you have. What you give is therefore the value you put on what you have, being the exact measure of the value you put upon it. And this, in turn, is the measure of how much you want it. (T-9.II.11:4-9)

> "Pilate therefore said unto him, Art thou a king then? Jesus answered, Thou sayest that I am a king. To this end was I born, and for this cause I came into the world, that I should bear witness unto the truth. Every one that is of the truth heareth my voice." (John 18:37)

> "But when the Comforter is come, whom I will send unto you from the Father, [even] the Spirit of truth, which proceedeth from the Father, he shall testify of me: And ye also shall bear witness, because ye have been with me from the beginning." (John 15:26-27)

Miracles bear witness to truth. They are convincing because they arise from conviction. (T-1.I.14:1-2)

I assure you that I will witness for anyone who lets me, and to whatever extent he permits it. Your witnessing demonstrates your belief, and thus strengthens it. Those who witness for me are expressing, through their miracles, that they have abandoned the belief in deprivation in favor of the abundance they have learned belongs to them. (T-1.IV.4:6-8)

> "They on the rock [are they], which, when they hear, receive the word with joy; and these have no root, which for a while believe, and in time of temptation fall away." (Luke 8:13)

The miracle is a sign that the mind has chosen to be led by me in Christ's service. The abundance of Christ is the natural result of choosing to follow Him. All shallow roots must be uprooted, because they are not deep enough to sustain you. (T-1.V.6:1-3)

> "For I was an hungered, and ye gave me meat: I was thirsty, and ye gave me drink: I was a stranger, and ye took me in." (Matthew 25:35)

As an expression of what you truly are, the miracle places the mind in a state of grace. The mind then naturally welcomes the Host within and the stranger without. When you bring in the stranger, he becomes your brother. (T-1.III.7:4-6)

> "And when he had called unto him his twelve disciples, he gave them power against unclean spirits, to cast them out, and to heal all manner of sickness and all manner of disease." (Matthew 10:1)

> "Heal the sick, cleanse the lepers, raise the dead, cast out devils: freely ye have received, freely give." (Matthew 10:8)

Miracles enable you to heal the sick and raise the dead because you made sickness and death yourself, and can therefore abolish both. *You* are a miracle, capable of creating in the likeness of your Creator. Everything else is your own nightmare, and does not exist. Only the creations of light are real. (T-1.I.24:1-4)

Ultimately, every member of the family of God must return. The miracle calls him to return because it blesses and honors him, even though he may be absent in spirit. "God is not mocked" is not a warning but a reassurance. God *would* be mocked if any of His creations lacked holiness. The creation is whole, and the mark of wholeness is holiness. Miracles are affirmations of Sonship, which is a state of completion and abundance. (T-1.V.4:1-6)

God is not mocked; no more His Son can be imprisoned save by his own desire. And it is by his own desire that he is freed. Such is his strength, and not his weakness. He is at his own mercy. And where he chooses to be merciful, there is he free. (T-21.VI.11:5-9)

Speak on the Beatitudes

> "And he opened his mouth, and taught them, saying, Blessed are the poor in spirit: for theirs is the kingdom of heaven." (Matthew 5:3)

Remember that those who attack are poor. Their poverty asks for gifts, not for further impoverishment. You who could help them are surely acting destructively if you accept their poverty as yours. (T-12.III.3:3-5)

> "Blessed are they that mourn: for they shall be comforted." (Matthew 5:4)

And let your gratitude make room for all who will escape with you; the sick, the weak, the needy and afraid, and those who mourn a seeming loss or feel apparent pain, who suffer cold or hunger, or who walk the way of hatred and the path of death. All these go with you. Let us not compare ourselves with them, for thus we split them off from our awareness of the unity we share with them, as they must share with us. (W-195.5:2-4)

We thank our Father for one thing alone; that we are separate from no living thing, and therefore one with Him. (W-195.6:1)

> "Blessed are the meek: for they shall inherit the earth." (Matthew 5:5)

The meek shall inherit the earth because their egos are humble, and this gives them truer perception. The Kingdom of Heaven is the spirit's right, whose beauty and dignity are far beyond doubt, beyond perception, and stand forever as the mark of the Love of God for His creations, who are wholly worthy of Him and only of Him. Nothing else is sufficiently worthy to be a gift for a creation of God Himself. (T-4.I.12:4-6)

> "Blessed are they which do hunger and thirst after righteousness: for they shall be filled." (Matthew 5:6)

... reach out to everyone who thirsts for living water, ... (T-18.VIII.9:8)

Go out and find them, for they bring your Self with them. And lead them gently to your quiet garden, and receive their blessing there. (T-18.VIII.10:1-2)

> "Blessed are the merciful: for they shall obtain mercy." (Matthew 5:7)

Sacrificing in any way is a violation of my injunction that you should be merciful even as your Father in Heaven is merciful. It has been hard for many Christians to realize that this applies to themselves. Good teachers never terrorize their students. (T-3.I.4:3-5)

> "Blessed are the pure in heart: for they shall see God." (Matthew 5:8)

The innocent see safety, and the pure in heart see God within His Son, and look unto the Son to lead them to the Father. And where else would they go but where they will to be? You and your brother now will lead the other to the Father as surely as God created His Son holy, and kept him so. In your brother is the light of God's eternal promise of your immortality. See him as sinless, and there can *be* no fear in you. (T-20.III.11:5-9)

Nothing can shake God's conviction of the perfect purity of everything that He created, for it *is* wholly pure. (T-14.III.12:2)

> "Blessed are the peacemakers: for they shall be called the children of God." (Matthew 5:9)

In every child of God His blessing lies, and in your blessing of the children of God is His blessing to you. (T-12.VII.1:6)

Everyone in the world must play his part in its redemption, in order to recognize that the world has been redeemed. (T-12.VII.2:1)

What Is the Devil?

"Then was Jesus led up of the Spirit into the wilderness to be tempted of the devil. And when he had fasted forty days and forty nights, he was afterward and hungered. And when the tempter came to him, he said, If thou be the Son of God, command that these stones be made bread. But he answered and said, It is written, Man shall not live by bread alone, but by every word that proceedeth out of the mouth of God.

Then the devil taketh him up into the holy city, and setteth him on a pinnacle of the temple, And saith unto him, If thou be the Son of God, cast thyself down: for it is written, He shall give his angels charge concerning thee: and in their hands they shall bear thee up, lest at any time thou dash thy foot against a stone. Jesus said unto him, It is written again, Thou shalt not tempt the Lord thy God. Again, the devil taketh him up into an exceeding high mountain, and showeth him all the kingdoms of the world, and the glory of them; And saith unto him, All these things will I give thee, if thou wilt fall down and worship me. Then saith Jesus unto him, Get thee hence, Satan: for it is written, Thou shalt worship the Lord thy God, and him only shalt thou serve. Then the devil leaveth him, and, behold, angels came and ministered unto him." (Matthew 4:1-11)

"And the great dragon was cast out, that old serpent, called the Devil, and Satan, which deceiveth the whole world: he was cast out into the earth, and his angels were cast out with him. And I heard a loud voice saying in heaven, Now is come salvation, and strength, and the kingdom of our God, and the power of his Christ: for the accuser of our brethren is cast down, which accused them before our God day and night." (Revelation 12:9-10)

The "devil" is a frightening concept because he seems to be extremely powerful and extremely active. He is perceived as a force in combat with God, battling Him for possession of His creations. The devil deceives by lies, and builds kingdoms in which everything is in direct opposition to God. Yet he attracts men rather than repels them, and they are willing to "sell" him their souls in return for gifts of no real worth. This makes absolutely no sense. (T-3.VII.2:4-8)

The mind can make the belief in separation very real and very fearful, and this belief *is* the "devil." It is powerful, active, destructive and clearly in opposition to God, because it literally denies His Fatherhood. Look at your life and see what the devil has made. But realize that this making will surely dissolve in the light of truth, because its foundation is a lie. Your creation by God is the only Foundation that cannot be shaken, because the light is in it. Your starting point is truth, and you must return to your Beginning. Much has been seen since then, but nothing has really happened. Your Self is still in peace, even though your mind is in conflict. You have not yet gone back far enough, and that is why you become so fearful. As you approach the Beginning, you feel the fear of the destruction of your thought system upon you as if it were the fear of death. There is no death, but there *is* a belief in death. (T-3.VII.5:1-11)

Accept Atonement with an open mind, which cherishes no lingering belief that you have made a devil of God's Son. There is no sin. We practice with this thought as often as we can today, because it is the basis for today's idea: (W-101.5:3-5)

God's Will for you is perfect happiness because there is no sin, and suffering is causeless. Joy is just, and pain is but the sign you have misunderstood yourself. Fear not the Will of God. (W-101.6:1-3)

What Is Temptation?

> "For in that he himself hath suffered being tempted, he is able to succour them that are tempted." (Hebrews 2:18)

I will substitute for your ego if you wish, but never for your spirit. A father can safely leave a child with an elder brother who has shown himself responsible, but this involves no confusion about the child's origin. The brother can protect the child's body and his ego, but he does not confuse himself with the father because he does this. I can be entrusted with your body and your ego only because this enables you not to be concerned with them, and lets me teach you their unimportance. I could not understand their importance to you if I had not once been tempted to believe in them myself. Let us undertake to learn this lesson together so we can be free of them together. I need devoted teachers who share my aim of healing the mind. Spirit is far beyond the need of your protection or mine. Remember this:

In this world you need not have tribulation because I have overcome the world. That is why you should be of good cheer. (T-4.I.13:1-11)

When you are tempted to yield to the desire for death, remember that I did not die. You will realize that this is true when you look within and see me. Would I have overcome death for myself alone? And would eternal life have been given me of the Father unless He had also given it to you? When you learn to make me manifest, you will never see death. For you will have looked upon the deathless in yourself, and you will see only the eternal as you look out upon a world that cannot die. (T-12.VII.15:1-6)

In me you have already overcome every temptation that would hold you back. We walk together on the way to quietness that is the gift of God. Hold me dear, for what except your brothers can you need? We will restore to you the peace of mind that we must find together. The Holy Spirit will teach you to awaken unto us and to yourself. This is the only real need to be fulfilled in time. Salvation from the world lies only here. My peace I give you. Take it of me in glad exchange for all the world has offered but to take away. And we will spread it like a veil of light across the world's sad face, in which we hide our brothers from the world, and it from them. (T-13.VII.16:1-10)

> "And lead us not into temptation, but deliver us from evil: For thine is the kingdom, and the power, and the glory, forever. Amen." (Matthew 6:13)

"Lead us not into temptation" means "Recognize your errors and choose to abandon them by following my guidance." (T-1.III.4:7)

Forgive us our illusions, Father, and help us to accept our true relationship with You, in which there are no illusions, and where none can ever enter. Our holiness is Yours. What can there be in us that needs forgiveness when Yours is perfect? The sleep of forgetfulness is only the unwillingness to remember Your forgiveness and Your Love. Let us not wander into temptation, for the temptation of the Son of God is not Your Will. And let us receive only what You have given, and accept but this unto the minds which You created and which You love. Amen. (T-16.VII.12:1-7)

Let us not let littleness lead God's Son into temptation. His glory is beyond it, measureless and timeless as eternity. Do not let time intrude upon your sight of him. Leave him not frightened and alone in his temptation, but help him rise above it and perceive the light of which he is a part. Your innocence will light the way to his, and so is yours protected and kept in your awareness. For who can know his glory, and perceive the little and the weak about him? Who can walk trembling in a fearful world, and realize that Heaven's glory shines on him? (T-23.in.5:1-7)

Temptation has one lesson it would teach, in all its forms, wherever it occurs. It would persuade the holy Son of God he is a body, born in what must die, unable to escape its frailty, and bound by what it orders him to feel. It sets the limits on what he can do; its power is the only strength he has; his grasp cannot exceed its tiny reach. Would you be this, if Christ appeared to you in all His glory, asking you but this:

Choose once again if you would take your place
among the saviors of the world, or would remain in
hell, and hold your brothers there.

For He *has* come, and He *is* asking this. (T-31.VIII.1:1-6)

> "Let no man say when he is tempted, I am tempted of God: for God cannot be tempted with evil, neither tempteth he any man:

> But every man is tempted, when he is drawn away of his own lust, and enticed. Then when lust hath conceived, it bringeth forth sin: and sin, when it is finished, bringeth forth death. Do not err, my beloved brethren. Every good gift and every perfect gift is from above, and cometh down from the Father of lights, with whom is no variableness, neither shadow of turning." (James 1:13-17)

When you are tempted to believe that sin is real, remember this: If sin is real, Both God and you are not. If creation is extension, the Creator must have extended Himself, and it is impossible that what is part of Him is totally unlike the rest. If sin is real, God must be at war with Himself. He must be split, and torn between good and evil; partly sane and partially insane. For He must have created what wills to destroy Him, and has the power to do so. Is it not easier to believe that you have been mistaken than to believe in this? (T-19.III.6:1-6)

The Kingdom is perfectly united and perfectly protected, and the ego will not prevail against it. Amen. (T-4.III.1:12-13)

This is written in the form of a prayer because it is useful in moments of temptation. It is a declaration of independence. You will find it very helpful if you understand it fully. (T-4.III.2:1-3)

Remember all temptation is but this; a mad belief that God's insanity would make you sane and give you what you want; that either God or you must lose to madness because your aims can not be reconciled. (T-25.VII.13:1)

Beware of the temptation to perceive yourself unfairly treated. In this view, you seek to find an innocence that is not Theirs but yours alone, and at the cost of someone else's guilt. Can innocence be purchased by the giving of your guilt to someone else? And *is* it innocence that your attack on him attempts to get? Is it not retribution for your own attack upon the Son of God you seek? Is it not safer to believe that you are innocent of this, and victimized despite your innocence? Whatever way the game of guilt is played, there must be loss. Someone must lose his innocence that someone else can take it from him, making it his own. (T-26.X.4:1-8)

You think your brother is unfair to you because you think that one must be unfair to make the other innocent. (T-26.X.5:1)

What is temptation but a wish to make illusions real? It does not seem to be the wish that no reality be so. Yet it is an assertion that some forms of idols have a powerful appeal that makes them harder to resist than those you would not want to have reality. Temptation, then, is nothing more than this; a prayer the miracle touch not some dreams, but keep their unreality obscure and give to them reality instead. And Heaven gives no answer to the prayer, nor can a miracle be given you to heal appearances you do not like. You have established limits. What you ask *is* given you, but not of God Who knows no limits. You have limited yourself. (T-30.VIII.3:1-8)

Reality is changeless. Miracles but show what you have interposed between reality and your awareness is unreal, and does not interfere at all. The cost of the belief there must be some appearances beyond the hope of change is that the miracle cannot come forth from you consistently. For you have asked it be withheld from power to heal all dreams. There is no miracle you cannot have when you desire healing. But there is no miracle that can be given you unless you want it. (T-30.VIII.4:1-6)

What is temptation but a wish to make the wrong decision on what you would learn, and have an outcome that you do not want? (T-31.I.11:1)

What is temptation but the wish to stay in hell and misery? And what could this give rise to but an image of yourself that can be miserable, and remain in hell and torment? (T-31.VII.10:1-2)

Be vigilant against temptation, then, remembering that it is but a wish, insane and meaningless, to make yourself a thing that you are not. And think as well upon the thing that you would be instead. It is a thing of madness, pain and death; a thing of treachery and black despair, of failing dreams and no remaining hope except to die, and end the dream of fear. *This* is temptation; nothing more than this. Can this be difficult to choose *against?* Consider what temptation is, and see the real alternatives you choose between. There are but two. Be not deceived by what appears as many choices. There is hell or Heaven, and of these you choose but one. (T-31.VII.14:1-9)

The images you make cannot prevail against what God Himself would have you be. Be never fearful of temptation, then, but see it as it is; another chance to choose again, and let Christ's strength prevail in every circumstance and every place you raised an image of yourself before. For what appears to hide the face of Christ is powerless before His majesty, and disappears before His holy sight. The saviors of the world, who see like Him, are merely those who choose His strength instead of their own weakness, seen apart from Him. They will redeem the world, for they are joined in all the power of the Will of God. And what they will is only what He wills. (T-31.VIII.4:1-6)

Learn, then, the happy habit of response to all temptation to perceive yourself as weak and miserable with these words:

I am as God created me. His Son can suffer nothing.
And I am His Son. (T-31.VIII.5:1-4)

> "And they came over unto the other side of the sea, into the country of the Gadarenes. And when he was come out of the ship, immediately there met him out of the tombs a man with an unclean spirit, Who had his dwelling among the tombs; and no man could bind him, no, not with chains: Because that he had been often bound with fetters and chains, and the chains had been plucked asunder by him, and the fetters broken in pieces: neither could any man tame him. And always, night and day, he was in the mountains, and in the tombs, crying, and cutting himself with stones.
>
> But when he saw Jesus afar off, he ran and worshipped him, And cried with a loud voice, and said, What have I to do with thee, Jesus, thou Son of the most high God? I adjure thee by God, that thou torment me not. For he said unto him, Come out of the man, thou unclean spirit. And he asked him, What is thy name? And he answered, saying, My name is Legion: for we are many." (Mark 5:1-9)

The ego is legion, but the Holy Spirit is One. No darkness abides anywhere in the Kingdom, but your part is only to allow no darkness to abide in your own mind. This alignment with light is unlimited, because it is in alignment with the light of the world. Each of us is the light of the world, and by joining our minds in this light we proclaim the Kingdom of God together and as one. (T-6.II.13:2-5)

Speak on Perfect Equality

"For the kingdom of heaven is like unto a man that is a householder, which went out early in the morning to hire labourers into his vineyard. And when he had agreed with the labourers for a penny a day, he sent them into his vineyard.

And he went out about the third hour, and saw others standing idle in the marketplace, And said unto them; Go ye also into the vineyard, and whatsoever is right I will give you. And they went their way. Again he went out about the sixth and ninth hour, and did likewise. And about the eleventh hour he went out, and found others standing idle, and saith unto them, Why stand ye here all the day idle? They say unto him, Because no man hath hired us. He saith unto them, Go ye also into the vineyard; and whatsoever is right, that shall ye receive. So when even was come, the lord of the vineyard saith unto his steward, Call the labourers, and give them their hire, beginning from the last unto the first.

And when they came that were hired about the eleventh hour, they received every man a penny. But when the first came, they supposed that they should have received more; and they likewise received every man a penny. And when they had received it, they murmured against the goodman of the house, Saying, These last have wrought but one hour, and thou hast made them equal unto us, which have borne the burden and heat of the day.

But he answered one of them, and said, Friend, I do thee no wrong: didst not thou agree with me for a penny? Take that thine is, and go thy way: I will give unto this last, even as unto thee.

Is it not lawful for me to do what I will with mine own? Is thine eye evil, because I am good?" (Matthew 20:1-15)

There is no order of difficulty in miracles. One is not "harder" or "bigger" than another. They are all the same. All expressions of love are maximal. (T-1.I.1:1-4)

Whatever lies you may believe are of no concern to the miracle, which can heal any of them with equal ease. It makes no distinctions among misperceptions. Its sole concern is to distinguish between truth on the one hand, and error on the other. Some miracles may seem to be of greater magnitude than others. But remember the first principle in this course; there is no order of difficulty in miracles. (T-2.I.5:1-5)

Unless the healer heals himself, he cannot believe that there is no order of difficulty in miracles. He has not learned that every mind God created is equally worthy of being healed *because* God created it whole. You are merely asked to return to God the mind as He created it. He asks you only for what He gave, knowing that this giving will heal you. Sanity is wholeness, and the sanity of your brothers is yours. (T-5.VII.2:4-8)

To the Holy Spirit, there is no order of difficulty in miracles. This is familiar enough to you by now, but it has not yet become believable. Therefore, you do not understand it and cannot use it. We have too much to accomplish on behalf of the Kingdom to let this crucial concept slip away. It is a real foundation stone of the thought system I teach and want you to teach. You cannot perform miracles without believing it, because it is a belief in perfect equality. Only one equal gift can be offered to the equal Sons of God, and that is full appreciation. Nothing more and nothing less. Without a range, order of difficulty is meaningless, and there must be no range in what you offer to your brother. (T-6.V.A.4:1-9)

The miracles the Holy Spirit inspires can have no order of difficulty, because every part of creation is of one order. This is God's Will and yours. The laws of God establish this, and the Holy Spirit reminds you of it. (T-7.IV.2:3-5)

By demonstrating to yourself there is no order of difficulty in miracles, you will convince yourself that, in your natural state, there is no difficulty at all *because* it is a state of grace. (T-7.XI.1:8)

There is no order of difficulty in miracles because all of God's Sons are of equal value, and their equality is their oneness. The whole power of God is in every part of Him, and nothing contradictory to His Will is either great or small. (T-11.VI.10:5-6)

You will recognize that you have learned there is no order of difficulty in miracles when you apply them to all situations. There is no situation to which miracles do not apply, and by applying them to all situations you will gain the real world. For in this holy perception you will be made whole, and the Atonement will radiate from your acceptance of it for yourself to everyone the Holy Spirit sends you for your blessing. In every child of God His blessing lies, and in your blessing of the children of God is His blessing to you. (T-12.VII.1:3-6)

It will seem difficult for you to learn that you have no basis at all for ordering your thoughts. This lesson the Holy Spirit teaches by giving you the shining examples of miracles to show you that your way of ordering is wrong, but that a better way is offered you. The miracle offers exactly the same response to every call for help. It does not judge the call. It merely recognizes what it is, and answers accordingly. It does not consider which call is louder or greater or more important. You may wonder how you who are still bound to judgment can be asked to do that which requires no judgment of your own. The answer is very simple. The power of God, and not of you, engenders miracles. The miracle itself is but the witness that you have the power of God in you. That is the reason why the miracle gives equal blessing to all who share in it, and that is also why everyone shares in it. The power of God is limitless. And being always maximal, it offers everything to every call from anyone. There is no order of difficulty here. (T-14.X.6:1-14)

Projection makes perception. The world you see is what you gave it, nothing more than that. But though it is no more than that, it is not less. Therefore, to you it is important. It is the witness to your state of mind, the outside picture of an inward condition. As a man thinketh, so does he perceive. Therefore, seek not to change the world, but choose to change your mind about the world. Perception is a result and not a cause. And that is why order of difficulty in miracles is meaningless. Everything looked upon with vision is healed and holy. Nothing perceived without it means anything. (T-21.in.1:1-11)

The miracle substitutes for learning that might have taken thousands of years. It does so by the underlying recognition of perfect equality of giver and receiver on which the miracle rests. (T-1.II.6:7-8)

What happens to perceptions if there are no judgments and nothing but perfect equality? Perception becomes impossible. Truth can only be known. All of it is equally true, and knowing any part of it is to know all of it. (T-3.V.8:1-4)

The Holy Spirit begins by perceiving you as perfect. Knowing this perfection is shared He recognizes it in others, thus strengthening it in both. Instead of anger this arouses love for both, because it establishes inclusion. Perceiving equality, the Holy Spirit perceives equal needs. This invites Atonement automatically, because Atonement is the one need in this world that is universal. To perceive yourself this way is the only way in which you can find happiness in the world. That is because it is the acknowledgment that you are not in this world, for the world *is* unhappy. (T-6.II.5:1-7)

The perfect equality of the Holy Spirit's perception is the reflection of the perfect equality of God's knowing. The ego's perception has no counterpart in God, but the Holy Spirit remains the Bridge between perception and knowledge. By enabling you to use perception in a way that reflects knowledge, you will ultimately remember it. (T-6.II.7:1-3)

Speak on Charity

> "Though I speak with the tongues of men and of angels, and have not charity, I am become as sounding brass, or a tinkling cymbal. And though I have the gift of prophecy, and understand all mysteries, and all knowledge; and though I have all faith, so that I could remove mountains, and have not charity, I am nothing. And though I bestow all my goods to feed the poor, and though I give my body to be burned, and have not charity, it profiteth me nothing. Charity suffereth long, and is kind; charity envieth not; charity vaunteth not itself, is not puffed up, Doth not behave itself unseemly, seeketh not her own, is not easily provoked, thinketh no evil;
>
> Rejoiceth not in iniquity, but rejoiceth in the truth; Beareth all things, believeth all things, hopeth all things, endureth all things. Charity never faileth." (1 Corinthians 13:1-8)

This is because healing rests on charity, and charity is a way of perceiving the perfection of another even if you cannot perceive it in yourself. Most of the loftier concepts of which you are capable now are time-dependent. Charity is really a weaker reflection of a much more powerful love-encompassment that is far beyond any form of charity you can conceive of as yet. Charity is essential to right-mindedness in the limited sense in which it can now be attained. (T-2.V.9:4-7)

Charity is a way of looking at another as if he had already gone far beyond his actual accomplishments in time. Since his own thinking is faulty he cannot see the Atonement for himself, or he would have no need of charity. The charity that is accorded him is both an acknowledgment that he needs help, and a recognition that he will accept it. Both of these perceptions clearly imply their dependence on time, making it apparent that charity still lies within the limitations of this world. I said before that only revelation transcends time. The miracle, as an expression of charity, can only shorten it. It must be understood, however, that whenever you offer a miracle to another, you are shortening the suffering of both of you. (T-2.V.10:1-7)

What Does It Mean to Be Still?

> "Be still, and know that I am God: I will be exalted among the heathen, I will be exalted in the earth." (Psalms 46:10)

You can speak from the spirit or from the ego, as you choose. If you speak from spirit you have chosen to "Be still and know that I am God." These words are inspired because they reflect knowledge. If you speak from the ego you are disclaiming knowledge instead of affirming it, and are thus dis-spiriting yourself. Do not embark on useless journeys, because they are indeed in vain. The ego may desire them, but spirit cannot embark on them because it is forever unwilling to depart from its Foundation. (T-4.in.2:1-6)

I am sorry when my brothers do not share my decision to hear only one Voice, because it weakens them as teachers and as learners. Yet I know they cannot really betray themselves or me, and that it is still on them that I must build my church. There is no choice in this, because only you can be the foundation of God's church. A church is where an altar is, and the presence of the altar is what makes the church holy. A church that does not inspire love has a hidden altar that is not serving the purpose for which God intended it. I must found His church on you, because those who accept me as a model are literally my disciples. Disciples are followers, and if the model they follow has chosen to save them pain in all respects, they are unwise not to follow him. (T-6.I.8:1-7)

This sacred Son of God is like yourself; the mirror of his Father's Love for you, the soft reminder of his Father's Love by which he was created and which still abides in him as it abides in you. Be very still and hear God's Voice in him, and let It tell you what his function is. He was created that you might be whole, for only the complete can be a part of God's completion, which created you. (T-29.V.4:1-3)

Be very still an instant. Come without all thought of what you ever learned before, and put aside all images you made. The old will fall away before the new without your opposition or intent. There will be no attack upon the things you thought were precious and in need of care. There will be no assault upon your wish to hear a call that never has been made. Nothing will hurt you in this holy place, to which you come to listen silently and learn the truth of what you really want. No more than this will you be asked to learn. But as you hear it, you will understand you need but come away without the thoughts you did not want, and that were never true. (T-31.II.8:1-8)

Does God Require Any Sacrifice?

> "For I desired mercy, and not sacrifice; and the knowledge of God more than burnt offerings." (Hosea 6:6)

> "Be ye therefore merciful, as your Father also is merciful." (Luke 6:36)

Sacrifice is a notion totally unknown to God. It arises solely from fear, and frightened people can be vicious. Sacrificing in any way is a violation of my injunction that you should be merciful even as your Father in Heaven is merciful. (T-3.I.4:1-3)

The innocence of God is the true state of the mind of His Son. In this state your mind knows God, for God is not symbolic; He is Fact. Knowing His Son as he is, you realize that the Atonement, not sacrifice, is the only appropriate gift for God's altar, where nothing except perfection belongs. The understanding of the innocent is truth. That is why their altars are truly radiant. (T-3.I.8:1-5)

At God's altar Christ waits for the restoration of Himself in you. God knows His Son as wholly blameless as Himself, and He is approached through the appreciation of His Son. Christ waits for your acceptance of Him as yourself, and of His Wholeness as yours. For Christ is the Son of God, Who lives in His Creator and shines with His glory. Christ is the extension of the Love and the loveliness of God, as perfect as His Creator and at peace with Him. (T-11.IV.7:1-5)

Blessed is the Son of God whose radiance is of his Father, and whose glory he wills to share as his Father shares it with him. There is no condemnation in the Son, for there is no condemnation in the Father. Sharing the perfect Love of the Father the Son must share what belongs to Him, for otherwise he will not know the Father or the Son. Peace be unto you who rest in God, and in whom the whole Sonship rests. (T-11.IV.8:1-4)

The statement "Vengeance is mine, sayeth the Lord" is a misperception by which one assigns his own "evil" past to God. The "evil" past has nothing to do with God. He did not create it and He does not maintain it. (T-3.I.3:1-3)

"Vengeance is mine, sayeth the Lord" is easily reinterpreted if you remember that ideas increase only by being shared. The statement emphasizes that vengeance cannot be shared. Give it therefore to the Holy Spirit, Who will undo it in you because it does not belong in your mind, which is part of God. (T-5.VI.7:1-3)

> "Let us hear the conclusion of the whole matter: Fear God, and keep his commandments: for this is the whole duty of man." (Ecclesiastes 12:13)

"Fear God and keep His commandments" becomes "Know God and accept His certainty." (T-3.III.6:7)

> "For the LORD is good; his mercy is everlasting; and his truth endureth to all generations." (Psalms 100:5)

> "Keeping mercy for thousands, forgiving iniquity and transgression and sin, and that will by no means clear the guilty; visiting the iniquity of the fathers upon the children, and upon the children's children, unto the third and to the fourth generation." (Exodus 34:7)

"I will visit the sins of the fathers unto the third and fourth generation," as interpreted by the ego, is particularly vicious. It becomes merely an attempt to guarantee the ego's own survival. To the Holy Spirit, the statement means that in later generations He can still reinterpret what former generations had misunderstood, and thus release the thoughts from the ability to produce fear. (T-5.VI.8:1-3)

> "But the wicked shall perish, and the enemies of the LORD shall be as the fat of lambs: they shall consume; into smoke shall they consume away." (Psalms 37:20)

"The wicked shall perish" becomes a statement of Atonement, if the word "perish" is understood as "be undone." Every loveless thought must be undone, a word the ego cannot even understand. To the ego, to be undone means to be destroyed. The ego will not be destroyed because it is part of your thought, but because it is uncreative and therefore unsharing, it will be reinterpreted to release you from fear. The part of your mind that you have given to the ego will merely return to the Kingdom, where your whole mind belongs. You can delay the completion of the Kingdom, but you cannot introduce the concept of fear into it. (T-5.VI.9:1-6)

> "For the wages of sin is death; but the gift of God is eternal life through Jesus Christ our Lord." (Romans 6:23)

Depression means that you have forsworn God. Many are afraid of blasphemy, but they do not understand what it means. They do not realize that to deny God is to deny their own Identity, and in this sense the wages of sin *is* death. The sense is very literal; denial of life perceives its opposite, as all forms of denial replace what is with what is not. No one can really do this, but that you can think you can and believe you have is beyond dispute. (T-10.V.1:3-7)

The Son of God can be mistaken; he can deceive himself; he can even turn the power of his mind against himself. But he *cannot* sin. There is nothing he can do that would really change his reality in any way, nor make him really guilty. That is what sin would do, for such is its purpose. Yet for all the wild insanity inherent in the whole idea of sin, it is impossible. For the wages of sin *is* death, and how can the immortal die? (T-19.II.3:1-6)

> "O Israel, trust thou in the LORD: he is their help and their shield." (Psalms 115:9)

Sickness and death seemed to enter the mind of God's Son against His Will. The "attack on God" made His Son think he was Fatherless, and out of his depression he made the god of depression. This was his alternative to joy, because he would not accept the fact that, although he was a creator, he had been created. Yet the Son *is* helpless without the Father, Who alone is his Help. (T-10.V.4:1-4)

What Is the Meaning of the Crucifixion?

> "When the morning was come, all the chief priests and elders of the people took counsel against Jesus to put him to death." (Matthew 27:1)

The crucifixion did not establish the Atonement; the resurrection did. Many sincere Christians have misunderstood this. No one who is free of the belief in scarcity could possibly make this mistake. If the crucifixion is seen from an upside-down point of view, it does appear as if God permitted and even encouraged one of His Sons to suffer because he was good. This particularly unfortunate interpretation, which arose out of projection, has led many people to be bitterly afraid of God. Such anti-religious concepts enter into many religions. Yet the real Christian should pause and ask, "How could this be?" Is it likely that God Himself would be capable of the kind of thinking which His Own words have clearly stated is unworthy of His Son? (T-3.I.1:2-9)

The journey to the cross should be the last "useless journey." Do not dwell upon it, but dismiss it as accomplished. If you can accept it as your own last useless journey, you are also free to join my resurrection. Until you do so your life is indeed wasted. It merely re-enacts the separation, the loss of power, the futile attempts of the ego at reparation, and finally the crucifixion of the body, or death. Such repetitions are endless until they are voluntarily given up. Do not make the pathetic error of "clinging to the old rugged cross." The only message of the crucifixion is that you can overcome the cross. (T-4.in.3:1-8)

There is a positive interpretation of the crucifixion that is wholly devoid of fear, and therefore wholly benign in what it teaches, if it is properly understood. (T-6.I.1:5)

The crucifixion is nothing more than an extreme example. Its value, like the value of any teaching device, lies solely in the kind of learning it facilitates. ... I have also told you that the crucifixion was the last useless journey the Sonship need take, and that it represents release from fear to anyone who understands it. ... Nevertheless, it has a definite contribution to make to your own life, and if you will consider it without fear, it will help you understand your own role as a teacher. (T-6.I.2:1-8)

You have probably reacted for years as if you were being crucified. This is a marked tendency of the separated, who always refuse to consider what they have done to themselves. Projection means anger, anger fosters assault, and assault promotes fear. The real meaning of the crucifixion lies in the *apparent* intensity of the assault of some of the Sons of God upon another. This, of course, is impossible, and must be fully understood *as* impossible. Otherwise, I cannot serve as a model for learning. (T-6.I.3:1-6)

Assault can ultimately be made only on the body. There is little doubt that one body can assault another, and can even destroy it. Yet if destruction itself is impossible, anything that is destructible cannot be real. Its destruction, therefore, does not justify anger. To the extent to which you believe that it does, you are accepting false premises and teaching them to others. The message the crucifixion was intended to teach was that it is not necessary to perceive any form of assault in persecution, because you cannot *be* persecuted. If you respond with anger, you must be equating yourself with the destructible, and are therefore regarding yourself insanely. (T-6.I.4:1-7)

I have made it perfectly clear that I am like you and you are like me, but our fundamental equality can be demonstrated only through joint decision. You are free to perceive yourself as persecuted if you choose. When you do choose to react that way, however, you might remember that I was persecuted as the world judges, and did not share this evaluation for myself. And because I did not share it, I did not strengthen it. I therefore offered a different interpretation of attack, and one which I want to share with you. If you will believe it, you will help me teach it. (T-6.I.5:1-6)

As I have said before, "As you teach so shall you learn." If you react as if you are persecuted, you are teaching persecution. This is not a lesson a Son of God should want to teach if he is to realize his own salvation. Rather, teach your own perfect immunity, which is the truth in you, and realize that it cannot *be* assailed. Do not try to protect it yourself, or you are believing that it is assailable. You are not asked to be crucified, which was part of my own teaching contribution. You are merely asked to follow my example in the face of much less extreme temptations to misperceive, and not to accept them as false justifications for anger. There can be no justification for the unjustifiable. Do not believe there is, and do not teach that there is. Remember always that what you believe you will teach. Believe with me, and we will become equal as teachers. (T-6.I.6:1-11)

Your resurrection is your reawakening. I am the model for rebirth, but rebirth itself is merely the dawning on your mind of what is already in it. God placed it there Himself, and so it is true forever. I believed in it, and therefore accepted it as true for me. Help me to teach it to our brothers in the name of the Kingdom of God, but first believe that it is true for you, or you will teach amiss. My brothers slept during the so-called "agony in the garden," but I could not be angry with them because I knew I could not *be* abandoned. (T-6.I.7:1-6)

I am sorry when my brothers do not share my decision to hear only one Voice, because it weakens them as teachers and as learners. Yet I know they cannot really betray themselves or me, and that it is still on them that I must build my church. There is no choice in this, because only you can be the foundation of God's church. A church is where an altar is, and the presence of the altar is what makes the church holy. A church that does not inspire love has a hidden altar that is not serving the purpose for which God intended it. I must found His church on you, because those who accept me as a model are literally my disciples. Disciples are followers, and if the model they follow has chosen to save them pain in all respects, they are unwise not to follow him. (T-6.I.8:1-7)

I elected, for your sake and mine, to demonstrate that the most outrageous assault, as judged by the ego, does not matter. As the world judges these things, but not as God knows them, I was betrayed, abandoned, beaten, torn, and finally killed. It was clear that this was only because of the projection of others onto me, since I had not harmed anyone and had healed many. (T-6.I.9:1-3)

When you hear only one Voice you are never called on to sacrifice. On the contrary, by being able to hear the Holy Spirit in others you can learn from their experiences, and can gain from them without experiencing them directly yourself. That is because the Holy Spirit is One, and anyone who listens is inevitably led to demonstrate His way for all. (T-6.I.10:4-6)

You are not persecuted, nor was I. (T-6.I.11:1)

The crucifixion cannot be shared because it is the symbol of projection, but the resurrection is the symbol of sharing because the reawakening of every Son of God is necessary to enable the Sonship to know its Wholeness. Only this is knowledge. (T-6.I.12:1-2)

The message of the crucifixion is perfectly clear:

Teach only love, for that is what you are. (T-6.I.13:1-2)

If you interpret the crucifixion in any other way, you are using it as a weapon for assault rather than as the call for peace for which it was intended. The Apostles often misunderstood it, and for the same reason that anyone misunderstands it. Their own imperfect love made them vulnerable to projection, and out of their own fear they spoke of the "wrath of God" as His retaliatory weapon. Nor could they speak of the crucifixion entirely without anger, because their sense of guilt had made them angry. (T-6.I.14:1-4)

These are some of the examples of upside-down thinking in the New Testament, although its gospel is really only the message of love. If the Apostles had not felt guilty, they never could have quoted me as saying, "I come not to bring peace but a sword." This is clearly the opposite of everything I taught. Nor could they have described my reactions to Judas as they did, if they had really understood me. I could not have said, "Betrayest thou the Son of man with a kiss?" unless I believed in betrayal. The whole message of the crucifixion was simply that I did not. The "punishment" I was said to have called forth upon Judas was a similar mistake. Judas was my brother and a Son of God, as much a part of the Sonship as myself. Was it likely that I would condemn him when I was ready to demonstrate that condemnation is impossible? (T-6.I.15:1-9)

As you read the teachings of the Apostles, remember that I told them myself that there was much they would understand later, because they were not wholly ready to follow me at the time. I do not want you to allow any fear to enter into the thought system toward which I am guiding you. I do not call for martyrs but for teachers. No one is punished for sins, and the Sons of God are not sinners. Any concept of punishment involves the projection of blame, and reinforces the idea that blame is justified. The result is a lesson in blame, for all behavior teaches the beliefs that motivate it. The crucifixion was the result of clearly opposed thought systems; the perfect symbol of the "conflict" between the ego and the Son of God. This conflict seems just as real now, and its lessons must be learned now as well as then. (T-6.I.16:1-8)

That is why you must teach only one lesson. If you are to be conflict-free yourself, you must learn only from the Holy Spirit and teach only by Him. You are only love, but when you deny this, you make what you are something you must learn to remember. I said before that the message of the crucifixion was, "Teach only love, for that is what you are." This is the one lesson that is perfectly unified, because it is the only lesson that is one. Only by teaching it can you learn it. "As you teach so will you learn." If that is true, and it is true indeed, do not forget that what you teach is teaching you. And what you project or extend you believe. (T-6.III.2:1-9)

Would you join in the resurrection or the crucifixion? Would you condemn your brothers or free them? Would you transcend your prison and ascend to the Father? These questions are all the same, and are answered together. There has been much confusion about what perception means, because the word is used both for awareness and for the interpretation of awareness. Yet you cannot be aware without interpretation, for what you perceive *is* your interpretation. (T-11.VI.2:1-6)

Do not underestimate the power of the devotion of God's Son, nor the power the god he worships has over him. For he places himself at the altar of his god, whether it be the god he made or the God Who created him. That is why his slavery is as complete as his freedom, for he will obey only the god he accepts. The god of crucifixion demands that he crucify, and his worshippers obey. In his name they crucify themselves, believing that the power of the Son of God is born of sacrifice and pain. The God of resurrection demands nothing, for He does not will to take away. He does not require obedience, for obedience implies submission. He would only have you learn your will and follow it, not in the spirit of sacrifice and submission, but in the gladness of freedom. (T-11.VI.5:1-8)

You will not find peace until you have removed the nails from the hands of God's Son, and taken the last thorn from his forehead. The Love of God surrounds His Son whom the god of crucifixion condemns. Teach not that I died in vain. Teach rather that I did not die by demonstrating that I live in you. For the undoing of the crucifixion of God's Son is the work of the redemption, in which everyone has a part of equal value. God does not judge His guiltless Son. Having given Himself to him, how could it be otherwise? (T-11.VI.7:1-7)

You have nailed yourself to a cross, and placed a crown of thorns upon your own head. Yet you cannot crucify God's Son, for the Will of God cannot die. His Son has been redeemed from his own crucifixion, and you cannot assign to death whom God has given eternal life. The dream of crucifixion still lies heavy on your eyes, but what you see in dreams is not reality. While you perceive the Son of God as crucified, you are asleep. And as long as you believe that you can crucify him, you are only having nightmares. You who are beginning to wake are still aware of dreams, and have not yet forgotten them. The forgetting of dreams and the awareness of Christ come with the awakening of others to share your redemption. (T-11.VI.8:1-8)

This world *is* a picture of the crucifixion of God's Son. And until you realize that God's Son cannot be crucified, this is the world you will see. Yet you will not realize this until you accept the eternal fact that God's Son is not guilty. He deserves only love because he has given only love. He cannot be condemned because he has never condemned. The Atonement is the final lesson he need learn, for it teaches him that, never having sinned, he has no need of salvation. (T-13.in.4:1-6)

The darkest of your hidden cornerstones holds your belief in guilt from your awareness. For in that dark and secret place is the realization that you have betrayed God's Son by condemning him to death. You do not even suspect this murderous but insane idea lies hidden there, for the ego's destructive urge is so intense that nothing short of the crucifixion of God's Son can ultimately satisfy it. It does not know who the Son of God is because it is blind. Yet let it perceive guiltlessness anywhere, and it will try to destroy it because it is afraid. (T-13.II.3:1-5)

I have said that the crucifixion is the symbol of the ego. When it was confronted with the real guiltlessness of God's Son it did attempt to kill him, and the reason it gave was that guiltlessness is blasphemous to God. To the ego, the *ego* is God, and guiltlessness must be interpreted as the final guilt that fully justifies murder. (T-13.II.6:1-3)

> "For God so loved the world, that he gave his only begotten Son, that whosoever believeth in him should not perish, but have everlasting life. For God sent not his Son into the world to condemn the world; but that the world through him might be saved." (John 3:16-17)

The statement "For God so loved the world that he gave his only begotten Son, that whosoever believeth in him should not perish but have everlasting life" needs only one slight correction to be meaningful in this context; "He gave it *to* His only begotten Son." (T-2.VII.5:14)

God does love the real world, and those who perceive its reality cannot see the world of death. For death is not of the real world, in which everything reflects the eternal. God gave you the real world in exchange for the one you made out of your split mind, and which is the symbol of death. For if you could really separate yourself from the Mind of God you would die. (T-12.III.8:2-5)

Speak on the Resurrection

A little while and you will see me, for I am not hidden because *you* are hiding. I will awaken you as surely as I awakened myself, for I awoke for you. In my resurrection is your release. Our mission is to escape from crucifixion, not from redemption. Trust in my help, for I did not walk alone, and I will walk with you as our Father walked with me. Do you not know that I walked with Him in peace? And does not that mean that peace goes with *us* on the journey? (T-12.II.7:1-7)

> "And, behold, there was a great earthquake: for the angel of the Lord descended from heaven, and came and rolled back the stone from the door, and sat upon it. His countenance was like lightning, and his raiment white as snow: And for fear of him the keepers did shake, and became as dead men. And the angel answered and said unto the women, Fear not ye: for I know that ye seek Jesus, which was crucified. He is not here: for he is risen, as he said. Come, see the place where the Lord lay.
>
> And go quickly, and tell his disciples that he is risen from the dead; and, behold, he goeth before you into Galilee; there shall ye see him: lo, I have told you. And they departed quickly from the sepulcher with fear and great joy; and did run to bring his disciples word.
>
> And as they went to tell his disciples, behold, Jesus met them, saying, All hail. And they came and held him by the feet, and worshipped him. Then said Jesus unto them, Be not afraid: go tell my brethren that they go into Galilee, and there shall they see me." (Matthew 28:2-10)

Jesus' response to Helen Shucman when she asked him whether he had a physical resurrection was, "My body disappeared because I had no illusion about it. The last one had gone. It was laid in the tomb, but there was nothing left to bury. It did not disintegrate because the unreal cannot die. It merely became what it always was. And that is what "rolling the stone away" means. The body disappears, and no longer hides what lies beyond.

It merely ceases to interfere with vision. To roll the stone away is to see beyond the tomb, beyond death, and to understand the body's nothingness. What is understood as nothing must disappear.

I did assume a human form with human attributes afterwards, to speak to those who were to prove the body's worthlessness to the world. This has been much misunderstood. I came to tell them that death is illusion, and the mind that made the body can make another since form itself is an illusion. They did not understand. But now I talk to you and give you the same message. The death of an illusion means nothing. It disappears when you awaken and decide to dream no more. And you still do have the power to make this decision as I did.

God holds out His hand to His Son to help him rise and return to Him. I can help because the world is an illusion, and I have overcome the world. Look past the tomb, the body, the illusion. Have faith in nothing but the spirit and the guidance God gives you. He could not have created the body because it is a limit. He must have created the spirit because it is immortal. Can those who are created like Him be limited? The body is the symbol of the world. Leave it behind. It cannot enter Heaven. But I can take you there any time you choose. Together we can watch the world disappear and its symbol vanish as it does so. And then, and then - I cannot speak of that.

A body cannot stay without illusion, and the last one to be overcome is death. This is the message of the crucifixion: There is no order of difficulty in miracles. This is the message of the resurrection: Illusions are illusions. Truth is true. Illusions vanish. Only truth remains.

These lessons needed to be taught but once, for when the stone of death is rolled away, what can be seen except an empty tomb? And that is what you see who follow Me into the sunlight and away from death, past all illusions, on to Heaven's gate, where God will come Himself to take you home."

(Kenneth Wapnick, *Absence from Felicity: the Story of Helen Shucman and Her Scribing of A Course in Miracles*)

Speak on the Last Judgment

> "For the Father judgeth no man, but hath committed all judgment unto the Son: That all men should honour the Son, even as they honour the Father. He that honoureth not the Son honoureth not the Father which hath sent him. Verily, verily, I say unto you, He that heareth my word, and believeth on him that sent me, hath everlasting life, and shall not come into condemnation; but is passed from death unto life.
>
> Verily, verily, I say unto you, The hour is coming, and now is, when the dead shall hear the voice of the Son of God: and they that hear shall live. For as the Father hath life in himself; so hath he given to the Son to have life in himself; And hath given him authority to execute judgment also, because he is the Son of man.
>
> Marvel not at this: for the hour is coming, in the which all that are in the graves shall hear his voice, And shall come forth; they that have done good, unto the resurrection of life." (John 5:22-29)
>
> "I heard a great voice of much people in heaven, saying, Alleluia; Salvation, and glory, and honour, and power, unto the Lord our God: For true and righteous are his judgments." (Revelation 19:2)
>
> "The LORD shall judge the people: judge me, O LORD, according to my righteousness, and according to mine integrity that is in me." (Psalms 7:8)

Your will to create was given you by your Creator, Who was expressing the same Will in His creation. Since creative ability rests in the mind, everything you create is necessarily a matter of will. It also follows that whatever you alone make is real in your own sight, though not in the Mind of God. This basic distinction leads directly into the real meaning of the Last Judgment. (T-2.VIII.1:3-6)

The Last Judgment is one of the most threatening ideas in your thinking. This is because you do not understand it. Judgment is not an attribute of God. It was brought into being only after the separation, when it became one of the many learning devices to be built into the overall plan. Just as the separation occurred over millions of years, the Last Judgment will extend over a similarly long period, and perhaps an even longer one. Its length can, however, be greatly shortened by miracles, the device for shortening but not abolishing time. If a sufficient number become truly miracle-minded, this shortening process can be virtually immeasurable. It is essential, however, that you free yourself from fear quickly, because you must emerge from the conflict if you are to bring peace to other minds. (T-2.VIII.2:1-8)

The Last Judgment is generally thought of as a procedure undertaken by God. Actually it will be undertaken by my brothers with my help. It is a final healing rather than a meting out of punishment, however much you may think that punishment is deserved. Punishment is a concept totally opposed to right-mindedness, and the aim of the Last Judgment is to restore right-mindedness to you. The Last Judgment might be called a process of right evaluation. It simply means that everyone will finally come to understand what is worthy and what is not. After this, the ability to choose can be directed rationally. Until this distinction is made, however, the vacillations between free and imprisoned will cannot but continue. (T-2.VIII.3:1-8)

The term "Last Judgment" is frightening not only because it has been projected onto God, but also because of the association of "last" with death. This is an outstanding example of upside-down perception. If the meaning of the Last Judgment is objectively examined, it is quite apparent that it is really the doorway to life. No one who lives in fear is really alive. Your own last judgment cannot be directed toward yourself, because you are not your own creation. You can, however, apply it meaningfully and at any time to everything you have made, and retain in your memory only what is creative and good. This is what your right-mindedness cannot but dictate. The purpose of time is solely to "give you time" to achieve this judgment. It is your own perfect judgment of your own perfect creations. When everything you retain is lovable, there is no reason for fear to remain with you. This is your part in the Atonement. (T-2.VIII.5:1-11)

The ego literally lives on borrowed time, and its days are numbered. Do not fear the Last Judgment, but welcome it and do not wait, for the ego's time is "borrowed" from your eternity. This is the Second Coming that was made for you as the First was created. The Second Coming is merely the return of sense. Can this possibly be fearful? (T-9.IV.9:1-5)

How Will the World End?

Can what has no beginning really end? The world will end in an illusion, as it began. Yet will its ending be an illusion of mercy. The illusion of forgiveness, complete, excluding no one, limitless in gentleness, will cover it, hiding all evil, concealing all sin and ending guilt forever. So ends the world that guilt had made, for now it has no purpose and is gone. The father of illusions is the belief that they have a purpose; that they serve a need or gratify a want. Perceived as purposeless, they are no longer seen. Their uselessness is recognized, and they are gone. How but in this way are all illusions ended? They have been brought to truth, and truth saw them not. It merely overlooked the meaningless. (M-14.1:1-11)

Until forgiveness is complete, the world does have a purpose. It becomes the home in which forgiveness is born, and where it grows and becomes stronger and more all-embracing. Here is it nourished, for here it is needed. A gentle Savior, born where sin was made and guilt seemed real. Here is His home, for here there is need of Him indeed. He brings the ending of the world with Him. It is His Call God's teachers answer, turning to Him in silence to receive His Word. The world will end when all things in it have been rightly judged by His judgment. The world will end with the benediction of holiness upon it. When not one thought of sin remains, the world is over. It will not be destroyed nor attacked nor even touched. It will merely cease to seem to be. (M-14.2:1-12)

Certainly this seems to be a long, long while away. "When not one thought of sin remains" appears to be a long-range goal indeed. But time stands still, and waits on the goal of God's teachers. Not one thought of sin will remain the instant any one of them accepts Atonement for himself. It is not easier to forgive one sin than to forgive all of them. The illusion of orders of difficulty is an obstacle the teacher of God must learn to pass by and leave behind. One sin perfectly forgiven by one teacher of God can make salvation complete. Can you understand this? No; it is meaningless to anyone here. Yet it is the final lesson in which unity is restored. It goes against all the thinking of the world, but so does Heaven. (M-14.3:1-11)

The world will end when its thought system has been completely reversed. Until then, bits and pieces of its thinking will still seem sensible. The final lesson, which brings the ending of the world, cannot be grasped by those not yet prepared to leave the world and go beyond its tiny reach. What, then, is the function of the teacher of God in this concluding lesson? He need merely learn how to approach it; to be willing to go in its direction. He need merely trust that, if God's Voice tells him it is a lesson he can learn, he can learn it. He does not judge it either as hard or easy. His Teacher points to it, and he trusts that He will show him how to learn it. (M-14.4:1-8)

The world will end in joy, because it is a place of sorrow. When joy has come, the purpose of the world has gone. The world will end in peace, because it is a place of war. When peace has come, what is the purpose of the world? The world will end in laughter, because it is a place of tears. Where there is laughter, who can longer weep? And only complete forgiveness brings all this to bless the world. In blessing it departs, for it will not end as it began. To turn hell into Heaven is the function of God's teachers, for what they teach are lessons in which Heaven is reflected. And now sit down in true humility, and realize that all God would have you do you can do. Do not be arrogant and say you cannot learn His Own curriculum. His Word says otherwise. His Will be done. It cannot be otherwise. And be you thankful it is so. (M-14.5:1-15)

What Is the Meaning of Bearing Fruit?

"He spake also this parable; A certain man had a fig tree planted in his vineyard; and he came and sought fruit thereon, and found none. Then said he unto the dresser of his vineyard, Behold, these three years I come seeking fruit on this fig tree, and find none: cut it down; why cumbereth it the ground? And he answering said unto him, Lord, let it alone this year also, till I shall dig about it, and dung it: And if it bear fruit, well: and if not, then after that thou shalt cut it down." (Luke 13:6-9)

"And he spake many things unto them in parables, saying, Behold, a sower went forth to sow; And when he sowed, some seeds fell by the way side, and the fowls came and devoured them up: Some fell upon stony places, where they had not much earth: and forthwith they sprung up, because they had no deepness of earth: And when the sun was up, they were scorched; and because they had no root, they withered away. And some fell among thorns; and the thorns sprung up, and choked them: But other fell into good ground, and brought forth fruit, some an hundredfold, some sixtyfold, some thirtyfold. Who hath ears to hear, let him hear." (Matthew 13:3-9)

"Hear ye therefore the parable of the sower. When any one heareth the word of the kingdom, and understandeth it not, then cometh the wicked one, and catcheth away that which was sown in his heart. This is he which received seed by the way side.

But he that received the seed into stony places, the same is he that heareth the word, and anon with joy receiveth it; Yet hath he not root in himself, but dureth for a while: for when tribulation or persecution ariseth because of the word, by and by he is offended.

He also that received seed among the thorns is he that heareth the word; and the care of this world, and the deceitfulness of riches, choke the word, and he becometh unfruitful.

> But he that received seed into the good ground is he that heareth the word, and understandeth it; which also beareth fruit, and bringeth forth, some an hundredfold, some sixty, some thirty." (Matthew 13:18-23)

> "Every branch in me that beareth not fruit he taketh away: and every branch that beareth fruit, he purgeth it, that it may bring forth more fruit." (John 15:2)

The branch that bears no fruit will be cut off and will wither away. Be glad! The light will shine from the true Foundation of life, and your own thought system will stand corrected. It cannot stand otherwise. You who fear salvation are choosing death. Life and death, light and darkness, knowledge and perception, are irreconcilable. To believe that they can be reconciled is to believe that God and His Son can *not.* Only the oneness of knowledge is free of conflict. Your Kingdom is not of this world because it was given you from beyond this world. Only in this world is the idea of an authority problem meaningful. The world is not left by death but by truth, and truth can be known by all those for whom the Kingdom was created, and for whom it waits. (T-3.VII.6:1-11)

Holy child of God, when will you learn that only holiness can content you and give you peace? Remember that you learn not for yourself alone, no more than I did. It is because I learned for you that you can learn of me. I would but teach you what is yours, so that together we can replace the shabby littleness that binds the host of God to guilt and weakness with the glad awareness of the glory that is in him. (T-15.III.9:1-4)

> "And Jesus said unto him, No man, having put his hand to the plow, and looking back, is fit for the kingdom of God." (Luke 9:62)

If you would be a happy learner, you must give everything you have learned to the Holy Spirit, to be unlearned for you. And then begin to learn the joyous lessons that come quickly on the firm foundation that truth is true. For what is builded there *is* true, and built on truth. The universe of learning will open up before you in all its gracious simplicity. With truth before you, you will not look back. (T-14.II.6:1-5)

> "Ye shall know them by their fruits. Do men gather grapes of thorns, or figs of thistles? Even so every good tree bringeth forth good fruit; but a corrupt tree bringeth forth evil fruit. A good tree cannot bring forth evil fruit, neither can a corrupt tree bring forth good fruit. Every tree that bringeth not forth good fruit is hewn down, and cast into the fire. Wherefore by their fruits ye shall know them." (Matthew 7:16-20)

> "Of his own will begat he us with the word of truth, that we should be a kind of first fruits of his creatures." (James 1:18)

> "Herein is my Father glorified, that ye bear much fruit; so shall ye be my disciples." (John 15:8)

> "Ye have not chosen me, but I have chosen you, and ordained you, that ye should go and bring forth fruit, and that your fruit should remain: that whatsoever ye shall ask of the Father in my name, he may give it you." (John 15:16)

This course offers a very direct and a very simple learning situation, and provides the Guide Who tells you what to do. If you do it, you will see that it works. Its results are more convincing than its words. They will convince you that the words are true. By following the right Guide, you will learn the simplest of all lessons:

By their fruits ye shall know them, and they shall know themselves. (T-9.V.9:1-6)

What Do These Sayings Mean?

> "And when Jesus had cried with a loud voice, he said, Father, into thy hands I commend my spirit." (Luke 23:46)

> "Beloved, now are we the sons of God, and it doth not yet appear what we shall be: but we know that, when he shall appear, we shall be like him; for we shall see him as he is." (1 John 3:2)

Nothing can prevail against a Son of God who commends his spirit into the Hands of his Father. By doing this the mind awakens from its sleep and remembers its Creator. All sense of separation disappears. The Son of God is part of the Holy Trinity, but the Trinity Itself is One. There is no confusion within Its Levels, because They are of one Mind and one Will. This single purpose creates perfect integration and establishes the peace of God. Yet this vision can be perceived only by the truly innocent. Because their hearts are pure, the innocent defend true perception instead of defending themselves against it. Understanding the lesson of the Atonement they are without the wish to attack, and therefore they see truly. This is what the Bible means when it says, "When he shall appear (or be perceived) we shall be like him, for we shall see him as he is." (T-3.II.5:1-10)

> "And whosoever shall compel thee to go a mile, go with him twain. Give to him that asketh thee, and from him that would borrow of thee turn not thou away. Ye have heard that it hath been said, Thou shalt love thy neighbour, and hate thine enemy. But I say unto you, Love your enemies, bless them that curse you, do good to them that hate you, and pray for them which despitefully use you, and persecute you; That ye may be the children of your Father which is in heaven: for he maketh his sun to rise on the evil and on the good, and sendeth rain on the just and on the unjust." (Matthew 5:41-45)

The Bible says that you should go with a brother twice as far as he asks. It certainly does not suggest that you set him back on his journey. Devotion to a brother cannot set you back either. It can lead only to mutual progress. The result of genuine devotion is inspiration, a word which properly understood is the opposite of fatigue. To be fatigued is to be dis-spirited, but to be inspired is to be in the spirit. To be egocentric is to be dis-spirited, but to be Self-centered in the right sense is to be inspired or in spirit. The truly inspired are enlightened and cannot abide in darkness. (T-4.in.1:1-8)

> "Therefore whosoever heareth these sayings of mine, and doeth them, I will liken him unto a wise man, which built his house upon a rock:
>
> And the rain descended, and the floods came, and the winds blew, and beat upon that house; and it fell not: for it was founded upon a rock.
>
> And every one that heareth these sayings of mine, and doeth them not, shall be likened unto a foolish man, which built his house upon the sand:
>
> And the rain descended, and the floods came, and the winds blew, and beat upon that house; and it fell: and great was the fall of it." (Matthew 7:24-27)
>
> "And he said unto me, My grace is sufficient for thee: for my strength is made perfect in weakness." (2 Corinthians 12:9)

The ego has built a shabby and unsheltering home for you, because it cannot build otherwise. Do not try to make this impoverished house stand. Its weakness is your strength. Only God could make a home that is worthy of His creations, who have chosen to leave it empty by their own dispossession. Yet His home will stand forever, and is ready for you when you choose to enter it. Of this you can be wholly certain. God is as incapable of creating the perishable as the ego is of making the eternal. (T-4.I.11:1-7)

> "Then answered Jesus and said unto them, Verily, verily, I say unto you, The Son can do nothing of himself, but what he seeth the Father do: for what things soever he doeth, these also doeth the Son likewise." (John 5:19)
>
> "For what is a man profited, if he shall gain the whole world, and lose his own soul? or what shall a man give in exchange for his soul?" (Matthew 16:26)

> "I can of mine own self do nothing: as I hear, I judge: and my judgment is just; because I seek not mine own will, but the will of the Father which hath sent Me." (John 5:30)

Of your ego you can do nothing to save yourself or others, but of your spirit you can do everything for the salvation of both. (T-4.I.12:1)

Rejoice, then, that of yourself you can do nothing. You are not *of* yourself. He of Whom you are has willed your power and glory for you, with which you can perfectly accomplish His holy Will for you when you accept it for yourself. He has not withdrawn His gifts from you, but you believe you have withdrawn them from Him. Let no Son of God remain hidden for His Name's sake, because His Name is yours. (T-8.VII.6:1-5)

> "Neither shall they say, Lo here! or, lo there! for, behold, the kingdom of God is within you." (Luke 17:21)

It is hard to understand what "The Kingdom of Heaven is within you" really means. This is because it is not understandable to the ego, which interprets it as if something outside is inside, and this does not mean anything. The word "within" is unnecessary. The Kingdom of Heaven *is* you. What else *but* you did the Creator create, and what else *but* you is His Kingdom? This is the whole message of the Atonement; a message which in its totality transcends the sum of its parts. You, too, have a Kingdom that your spirit created. It has not ceased to create because of the ego's illusions. Your creations are no more fatherless than you are. Your ego and your spirit will never be co-creators, but your spirit and your Creator will always be. (T-4.III.1:1-10)

Beautiful child of God, you are asking only for what I promised you. Do you believe I would deceive you? The Kingdom of Heaven *is* within you. Believe that the truth is in me, for I know that it is in you. (T-11.VIII.8:1-4)

The Kingdom of Heaven is the dwelling place of the Son of God, who left not his Father and dwells not apart from Him. Heaven is not a place nor a condition. It is merely an awareness of perfect Oneness, and the knowledge that there is nothing else; nothing outside this Oneness, and nothing else within. (T-18.VI.1:4-6)

> "For where two or three are gathered together in my name, there am I in the midst of them." (Matthew 18:20)

> "Again I say unto you, That if two of you shall agree on earth as touching any thing that they shall ask, it shall be done for them of my Father which is in heaven." (Matthew 18:19)

Healing is a thought by which two minds perceive their oneness and become glad. This gladness calls to every part of the Sonship to rejoice with them, and lets God go out into them and through them. (T-5.I.1:1-2)

You have done miracles, but it is quite apparent that you have not done them alone. You have succeeded whenever you have reached another mind and joined with it. When two minds join as one and share one idea equally, the first link in the awareness of the Sonship as One has been made. (T-16.II.4:1-3)

You have gone past fear, for no two minds can join in the desire for love without love's joining them. (T-18.III.7:7)

Two minds with one intent become so strong that what they will becomes the Will of God. For minds can only join in truth. (W-185.3:1-2)

I do not attack your ego. I do work with your higher mind, the home of the Holy Spirit, whether you are asleep or awake, just as your ego does with your lower mind, which is its home. I am your vigilance in this, because you are too confused to recognize your own hope. I am not mistaken. Your mind will elect to join with mine, and together we are invincible. You and your brother will yet come together in my name, and your sanity will be restored. (T-4.IV.11:1-6)

> "And when he thus had spoken, he cried with a loud voice, Lazarus, come forth. And he that was dead came forth, bound hand and foot with graveclothes: and his face was bound about with a napkin. Jesus saith unto them, Loose him, and let him go. Then many of the Jews which came to Mary, and had seen the things which Jesus did, believed on him." (John 11:43-45)

I raised the dead by knowing that life is an eternal attribute of everything that the living God created. Why do you believe it is harder for me to inspire the dis-spirited or to stabilize the unstable? I do not believe that there is an order of difficulty in miracles; you do. I have called and you will answer. I understand that miracles are natural, because they are expressions of love. My calling you is as natural as your answer, and as inevitable. (T-4.IV.11:7-12)

There have been many healers who did not heal themselves. They have not moved mountains by their faith because their faith was not whole. Some of them have healed the sick at times, but they have not raised the dead. Unless the healer heals himself, he cannot believe that there is no order of difficulty in miracles. He has not learned that every mind God created is equally worthy of being healed *because* God created it whole. You are merely asked to return to God the mind as He created it. He asks you only for what He gave, knowing that this giving will heal you. Sanity is wholeness, and the sanity of your brothers is yours. (T-5.VII.2:1-8)

> "And there shall be no more death, neither sorrow, nor crying, neither shall there be any more pain: for the former things are passed away." (Revelation 21:4)

The emptiness engendered by fear must be replaced by forgiveness. That is what the Bible means by "There is no death," and why I could demonstrate that death does not exist. (T-1.IV.4:1-2)

> "And we know that all things work together for good to them that love God, to them who are the called according to his purpose." (Romans 8:28)

All things work together for good. There are no exceptions except in the ego's judgment. (T-4.V.1:1-2)

> "Let this mind be in you, which was also in Christ Jesus." (Philippians 2:5)

This is the invitation to the Holy Spirit. I have said already that I can reach up and bring the Holy Spirit down to you, but I can bring Him to you only at your own invitation. The Holy Spirit is in your right mind, as He was in mine. The Bible says, "May the mind be in you that was also in Christ

Jesus," and uses this as a blessing. It is the blessing of miracle-mindedness. It asks that you may think as I thought, joining with me in Christ thinking. (T-5.I.3:1-6)

Remember the Kingdom always, and remember that you who are part of the Kingdom cannot be lost. The Mind that was in me *is* in you, for God creates with perfect fairness. Let the Holy Spirit remind you always of His fairness, and let me teach you how to share it with your brothers. How else can the chance to claim it for yourself be given you? The two voices speak for different interpretations of the same thing simultaneously; or almost simultaneously, for the ego always speaks first. Alternate interpretations were unnecessary until the first one was made. (T-5.VI.3:1-6)

> "Finally, be ye all of one mind, having compassion one of another, love as brethren, be pitiful, be courteous." (1 Peter 3:8)

> "This do in remembrance of me." (Luke 22:19)

The injunction "Be of one mind" is the statement for revelation-readiness. My request "Do this in remembrance of me" is the appeal for cooperation from miracle workers. The two statements are not in the same order of reality. Only the latter involves an awareness of time, since to remember is to recall the past in the present. Time is under my direction, but timelessness belongs to God. In time we exist for and with each other. In timelessness we coexist with God. (T-2.V.A.17:1-7)

> "And Jesus came and spake unto them, saying, All power is given unto me in heaven and in earth." (Matthew 28:18)

My mind will always be like yours, because we were created as equals. It was only my decision that gave me all power in Heaven and earth. My only gift to you is to help you make the same decision. This decision is the choice to share it, because the decision itself *is* the decision to share. It is made by giving, and is therefore the one choice that resembles true creation. I am your model for decision. By deciding for God I showed you that this decision can be made, and that you can make it. (T-5.II.9:1-7)

I have assured you that the Mind that decided for me is also in you, and that you can let it change you just as it changed me. This Mind is unequivocal, because it hears only one Voice and answers in only one way. You are the light of the world with me. Rest does not come from sleeping but from waking. The Holy Spirit is the Call to awaken and be glad. The world is very tired, because it is the idea of weariness. Our task is the joyous one of waking it to the Call for God. Everyone will answer the Call of the Holy Spirit, or the Sonship cannot be as One. What better vocation could there be for any part of the Kingdom than to restore it to the perfect integration that can make it whole? Hear only this through the Holy Spirit within you, and teach your brothers to listen as I am teaching you. (T-5.II.10:1-10)

If you will accept the fact that I am with you, you are denying the world and accepting God. My will is His, and your decision to hear me is the decision to hear His Voice and abide in His Will. As God sent me to you so will I send you to others. And I will go to them with you, so we can teach them peace and union. (T-8.IV.3:8-11)

> "Then spake Jesus again unto them, saying, I am the light of the world: he that followeth me shall not walk in darkness, but shall have the light of life." (John 8:12)

I am come as a light into a world that does deny itself everything. It does this simply by dissociating itself from everything. It is therefore an illusion of isolation, maintained by fear of the same loneliness that *is* its illusion. I said that I am with you always, even unto the end of the world. That is why I am the light of the world. If I am with you in the loneliness of the world, the loneliness is gone. You cannot maintain the illusion of loneliness if you are not alone. (T-8.IV.2:1-7)

> "Ye are the light of the world. A city that is set on an hill cannot be hid. Neither do men light a candle, and put it under a bushel, but on a candlestick; and it giveth light unto all that are in the house. Let your light so shine before men, that they may see your good works, and glorify your Father which is in heaven." (Matthew 5:14-16)

> "For there is nothing hid, which shall not be manifested; neither was any thing kept secret, but that it should come abroad. If any man have ears to hear, let him hear." (Mark 4:22-23)

> "Come unto me, all ye that labour and are heavy laden, and I will give you rest. Take my yoke upon you, and learn of me; for I am meek and lowly in heart: and ye shall find rest unto your souls. For my yoke is easy, and my burden is light." (Matthew 11:28-30)

Remember that "yoke" means "join together," and "burden" means "message." Let us restate "My yoke is easy and my burden light" in this way; "Let us join together, for my message is light." (T-5.II.11:3-4)

> "And ye shall know the truth, and the truth shall make you free." (John 8:32)

The ego made the world as it perceives it, but the Holy Spirit, the reinterpreter of what the ego made, sees the world as a teaching device for bringing you home. The Holy Spirit must perceive time, and reinterpret it into the timeless. He must work through opposites, because He must work with and for a mind that is in opposition. Correct and learn, and be open to learning. You have not made truth, but truth can still set you free. Look as the Holy Spirit looks, and understand as He understands. (T-5.III.11:1-6)

> "But I say unto you, That ye resist not evil: but whosoever shall smite thee on thy right cheek, turn to him the other also." (Matthew 5:39)

You cannot be hurt, and do not want to show your brother anything except your wholeness. Show him that he cannot hurt you and hold nothing against him, or you hold it against yourself. This is the meaning of "turning the other cheek." (T-5.IV.4:4-6)

> "Whatsoever a man soweth, that shall he also reap." (Galatians 6:7)

"As ye sow, so shall ye reap" He interprets to mean what you consider worth cultivating you will cultivate in yourself. Your judgment of what is worthy makes it worthy for you. (T-5.VI.6:1-2)

> "Take my yoke upon you, and learn of me." (Matthew 11:29)

Each one must learn to teach that all forms of rejection are meaningless. The separation is the notion of rejection. As long as you teach this you will believe it. This is not as God thinks, and you must think as He thinks if you are to know Him again. (T-6.I.18:3-6)

Remember that the Holy Spirit is the Communication Link between God the Father and His separated Sons. If you will listen to His Voice you will know that you cannot either hurt or be hurt, and that many need your blessing to help them hear this for themselves. When you perceive only this need in them, and do not respond to any other, you will have learned of me and will be as eager to share your learning as I am. (T-6.I.19:1-3)

> "And when all things shall be subdued unto him, then shall the Son also himself be subject unto him that put all things under him, that God may be all in all." (1 Corinthians 15:28)

God is All in all in a very literal sense. All being is in Him Who is all Being. You are therefore in Him since your being is His. (T-7.IV.7:4-6)

> "And to know the love of Christ, which passeth knowledge, that ye might be filled with all the fullness of God." (Ephesians 3:19)

Spirit knows that the awareness of all its brothers is included in its own, as it is included in God. The power of the whole Sonship and of its Creator is therefore spirit's own fullness, rendering its creations equally whole and equal in perfection. (T-7.IX.2:1-2)

> "For the LORD shall comfort Zion: he will comfort all her waste places; and he will make her wilderness like Eden, and her desert like the garden of the LORD; joy and gladness shall be found therein, thanksgiving, and the voice of melody." (Isaiah 51:3)

The Thought of God surrounds your little kingdom, waiting at the barrier you built to come inside and shine upon the barren ground. See how life springs up everywhere! The desert becomes a garden, green and deep and quiet, offering rest to those who lost their way and wander in the dust. Give them a place of refuge, prepared by love for them where once a desert was. And everyone you welcome will bring love with him from Heaven for you. They enter one by one into this holy place, but they will not depart as they had come, alone. The love they brought with them will stay with them, as it will stay with you. And under its beneficence your little garden will expand,

and reach out to everyone who thirsts for living water, but has grown too weary to go on alone. (T-18.VIII.9:1-8)

The blood of hatred fades to let the grass grow green again, and let the flowers be all white and sparkling in the summer sun. What was a place of death has now become a living temple in a world of light. Because of Them. It is Their Presence which has lifted holiness again to take its ancient place upon an ancient throne. Because of Them have miracles sprung up as grass and flowers on the barren ground that hate had scorched and rendered desolate. What hate has wrought have They undone. And now you stand on ground so holy Heaven leans to join with it, and make it like itself. The shadow of an ancient hate has gone, and all the blight and withering have passed forever from the land where They have come. (T-26.IX.3:1-8)

> "I will lift up mine eyes unto the hills, from whence cometh my help." (Psalms 121:1)

Your home has called to you since time began, nor have you ever failed entirely to hear. You heard, but knew not how to look, nor where. And now you know. In you the knowledge lies, ready to be unveiled and freed from all the terror that kept it hidden. There *is* no fear in love. The song of Easter is the glad refrain the Son of God was never crucified. Let us lift up our eyes together, not in fear but faith. And there will be no fear in us, for in our vision will be no illusions; only a pathway to the open door of Heaven, the home we share in quietness and where we live in gentleness and peace, as one together. (T-20.II.8:5-12)

The song of freedom, which sings the praises of another world, brings to it hope of peace. For it remembers Heaven, and now it sees that Heaven has come to earth at last, from which the ego's rule has kept it out so long. Heaven has come because it found a home in your relationship on earth. And earth can hold no longer what has been given Heaven as its own. (T-21.IV.7:4-7)

> "Pilate saith unto Jesus, What is truth?" (John 18:38)

Out of your natural environment you may well ask, "What is truth?" since truth is the environment by which and for which you were created. You do not know yourself, because you do not know your Creator. You do not know your creations because you do not know your brothers, who created them with you. (T-7.XI.6:1-3)

Can you be separated from your life and your being? The journey to God is merely the reawakening of the knowledge of where you are always, and what you are forever. It is a journey without distance to a goal that has never changed. Truth can only be experienced. It cannot be described and it cannot be explained. I can make you aware of the conditions of truth, but the experience is of God. Together we can meet its conditions, but truth will dawn upon you of itself. (T-8.VI.9:5-11)

If you do not know what your reality is, why would you be so sure that it is fearful? The association of truth and fear, which would be highly artificial at most, is particularly inappropriate in the minds of those who do not know what truth is. All this could mean is that you are arbitrarily associating something beyond your awareness with something you do not want. It is evident, then, that you are judging something of which you are totally unaware. (T-9.I.3:1-4)

You may insist that the Holy Spirit does not answer you, but it might be wiser to consider the kind of questioner you are. You do not ask only for what you want. This is because you are afraid you might receive it, and you would. That is why you persist in asking the teacher who could not possibly give you what you want. Of him you can never learn what it is, and this gives you the illusion of safety. Yet you cannot be safe *from* truth, but only *in* truth. Reality is the only safety. Your will is your salvation because it is the same as God's. The separation is nothing more than the belief that it is different. (T-9.I.7:1-9)

Ultimately everyone must remember the Will of God, because ultimately everyone must recognize himself. This recognition is the recognition that his will and God's are one. In the presence of truth, there are no unbelievers and no sacrifices. In the security of reality, fear is totally meaningless. (T-9.I.9:1-4)

You do not recognize the enormous waste of energy you expend in denying truth. What would you say of someone who persists in attempting the impossible, believing that to achieve it is to succeed? (T-9.I.11:1-2)

Remember, then, that God's Will is already possible, and nothing else will ever be. This is the simple acceptance of reality, because only that is real. You cannot distort reality and know what it is. And if you do distort reality you will experience anxiety, depression and ultimately panic, because you are trying to make yourself unreal. When you feel these things, do not try to look beyond yourself for truth, for truth can only be within you. (T-9.I.14:1-5)

The message your brother gives you is up to you. What does he say to you? What would you have him say? Your decision about him determines the message you receive. Remember that the Holy Spirit is in him, and His Voice speaks to you through him. What can so holy a brother tell you except truth? But are you listening to it? (T-9.II.5:1-7)

Believe in your brothers because I believe in you, and you will learn that my belief in you is justified. Believe in me *by* believing in them, for the sake of what God gave them. They will answer you if you learn to ask only truth of them. Do not ask for blessings without blessing them, for only in this way can you learn how blessed you are. By following this way you are seeking the truth in you. This is not going beyond yourself but toward yourself. Hear only God's Answer in His Sons, and you are answered. (T-9.II.8:1-7)

Remember this when the ego speaks, and you will not hear it. The truth about you is so lofty that nothing unworthy of God is worthy of you. Choose, then, what you want in these terms, and accept nothing that you would not offer to God as wholly fitting for Him. You do not want anything else. Return your part to Him, and He will give you all of Himself in exchange for the return of what belongs to Him and renders Him complete. (T-9.VII.8:3-7)

Yet if truth is indivisible, your evaluation of yourself must *be* God's. You did not establish your value and it needs no defense. Nothing can attack it nor prevail over it. It does not vary. It merely *is.* Ask the Holy Spirit what it is and He will tell you, but do not be afraid of His answer, because it comes from God. It is an exalted answer because of its Source, but the Source is true and so is Its answer. Listen and do not question what you hear, for God does not deceive. He would have you replace the ego's belief in littleness with His Own exalted Answer to what you are, so that you can cease to question it and know it for what it is. (T-9.VIII.11:1-9)

You will remember everything the instant you desire it wholly, for if to desire wholly is to create, you will have willed away the separation, returning your mind simultaneously to your Creator and your creations. Knowing Them you will have no wish to sleep, but only the desire to waken and be glad. Dreams will be impossible because you will want only truth, and being at last your will, it will be yours. (T-10.I.4:1-3)

> "Glory to God in the highest, and on earth peace, good will toward men." (Luke 2:14)

To what else except all power and glory can the Holy Spirit appeal to restore God's Kingdom? His appeal, then, is merely to what the Kingdom is, and for its own acknowledgment of what it is. When you acknowledge this you bring the acknowledgment automatically to everyone, because you *have* acknowledged everyone. By your recognition you awaken theirs, and through theirs yours is extended. Awakening runs easily and gladly through the Kingdom, in answer to the Call for God. This is the natural response of every Son of God to the Voice for his Creator, because It is the Voice for his creations and for his own extension. (T-8.II.8:1-6)

Glory to God in the highest, and to you because He has so willed it. (T-8.III.1:1)

To fulfill the Will of God perfectly is the only joy and peace that can be fully known, because it is the only function that can be fully experienced. When this is accomplished, then, there is no other experience. Yet the wish for other experience will block its accomplishment, because God's Will cannot be forced upon you, being an experience of total willingness. (T-8.III.2:1-3)

> "There was a certain rich man, which was clothed in purple and fine linen, and fared sumptuously every day: And there was a certain beggar named Lazarus, which was laid at his gate, full of sores, And desiring to be fed with the crumbs which fell from the rich man's table: moreover the dogs came and licked his sores.
>
> And it came to pass, that the beggar died, and was carried by the angels into Abraham's bosom: the rich man also died, and was buried; And in hell he lift up his eyes, being in torments, and seeth Abraham afar off, and Lazarus in his bosom. And he cried and said, Father Abraham, have mercy on me, and send Lazarus,

that he may dip the tip of his finger in water, and cool my tongue; for I am tormented in this flame.

But Abraham said, Son, remember that thou in thy lifetime receivedst thy good things, and likewise Lazarus evil things: but now he is comforted, and thou art tormented. And beside all this, between us and you there is a great gulf fixed: so that they which would pass from hence to you cannot; neither can they pass to us, that would come from thence.

Then he said, I pray thee therefore, father, that thou wouldest send him to my father's house: For I have five brethren; that he may testify unto them, lest they also come into this place of torment. Abraham saith unto him, They have Moses and the prophets; let them hear them. And he said, Nay, father Abraham: but if one went unto them from the dead, they will repent.

And he said unto him, If they hear not Moses and the prophets, neither will they be persuaded, though one rose from the dead." (Luke 16:19-31)

"Many are called but few are chosen" should be, "All are called but few choose to listen." Therefore, they do not choose right. The "chosen ones" are merely those who choose right sooner. Right minds can do this now, and they will find rest unto their souls. God knows you only in peace, and this *is* your reality. (T-3.IV.7:12-16)

The Call is universal. It goes on all the time everywhere. It calls for teachers to speak for It and redeem the world. Many hear It, but few will answer. Yet it is all a matter of time. Everyone will answer in the end, but the end can be a long, long way off. (M-1.2:4-9)

Speak on Time and the Meaning of Born Again

> "Behold, now is the accepted time; behold, now is the day of salvation." (2 Corinthians 6:2)

Now is the time of salvation, for now is the release from time. Reach out to all your brothers, and touch them with the touch of Christ. In timeless union with them is your continuity, unbroken because it is wholly shared. God's guiltless Son is only light. There is no darkness in him anywhere, for he is whole. Call all your brothers to witness to his wholeness, as I am calling you to join with me. Each voice has a part in the song of redemption, the hymn of gladness and thanksgiving for the light to the Creator of light. The holy light that shines forth from God's Son is the witness that his light is of his Father. (T-13.VI.8:1-8)

> "There was a man of the Pharisees, named Nicodemus, a ruler of the Jews: The same came to Jesus by night, and said unto him, Rabbi, we know that thou art a teacher come from God: for no man can do these miracles that thou doest, except God be with him.
>
> Jesus answered and said unto him, Verily, verily, I say unto thee, Except a man be born again, he cannot see the kingdom of God.
>
> Nicodemus saith unto him, How can a man be born when he is old? can he enter the second time into his mother's womb, and be born?
>
> Jesus answered, Verily, verily, I say unto thee, Except a man be born of water and of the Spirit, he cannot enter into the kingdom of God. That which is born of the flesh is flesh; and that which is born of the Spirit is spirit. Marvel not that I said unto thee, Ye must be born again.
>
> The wind bloweth where it listeth, and thou hearest the sound thereof, but canst not tell whence it cometh, and whither it goeth: so is every one that is born of the Spirit." (John 3:1-8)

> "No man also seweth a piece of new cloth on an old garment: else the new piece that filled it up taketh away from the old, and the rent is made worse. And no man putteth new wine into old bottles: else the new wine doth burst the bottles, and the wine is spilled, and the bottles will be marred: but new wine must be put into new bottles." (Mark 2:22)

The Christ as revealed to you now has no past, for He is changeless, and in His changelessness lies your release. For if He is as He was created, there is no guilt in Him. No cloud of guilt has risen to obscure Him, and He stands revealed in everyone you meet because you see Him through Himself. To be born again is to let the past go, and look without condemnation upon the present. The cloud that obscures God's Son to you *is* the past, and if you would have it past and gone, you must not see it now. If you see it now in your illusions, it has not gone from you, although it is not there. (T-13.VI.3:2-7)

Time can release as well as imprison, depending on whose interpretation of it you use. Past, present and future are not continuous, unless you force continuity on them. You can perceive them as continuous, and make them so for you. But do not be deceived, and then believe that this is how it is. For to believe reality is what you would have it be according to your use for it *is* delusional. You would destroy time's continuity by breaking it into past, present and future for your own purposes. You would anticipate the future on the basis of your past experience, and plan for it accordingly. Yet by doing so you are aligning past and future, and not allowing the miracle, which could intervene between them, to free you to be born again. (T-13.VI.4:1-8)

The miracle enables you to see your brother without his past, and so perceive him as born again. His errors are all past, and by perceiving him without them you are releasing him. And since his past is yours, you share in this release. Let no dark cloud out of your past obscure him from you, for truth lies only in the present, and you will find it if you seek it there. You have looked for it where it is not, and therefore have not found it. Learn, then, to seek it where it is, and it will dawn on eyes that see. Your past was made in anger, and if you use it to attack the present, you will not see the freedom that the present holds. (T-13.VI.5:1-7)

Determine, then, to be not as you were. Use no relationship to hold you to the past, but with each one each day be born again. A minute, even less, will be enough to free you from the past, and give your mind in peace over to the Atonement. When everyone is welcome to you as you would have yourself be welcome to your Father, you will see no guilt in you. For you will have accepted the Atonement, which shone within you all the while you dreamed of guilt, and would not look within and see it. (T-13.X.5:1-5)

Eternity is one time, its only dimension being "always." This cannot mean anything to you until you remember God's open Arms, and finally know His open Mind. Like Him, *you* are "always"; in His Mind and with a mind like His. (T-9.VI.7:1-2)

This lesson takes no time. For what is time without a past and future? It has taken time to misguide you so completely, but it takes no time at all to be what you are. Begin to practice the Holy Spirit's use of time as a teaching aid to happiness and peace. Take this very instant, now, and think of it as all there is of time. Nothing can reach you here out of the past, and it is here that you are completely absolved, completely free and wholly without condemnation. From this holy instant wherein holiness was born again you will go forth in time without fear, and with no sense of change with time. (T-15.I.9:1-7)

Yet every instant can you be reborn, and given life again. His holiness gives life to you, who cannot die because his sinlessness is known to God; and can no more be sacrificed by you than can the light in you be blotted out because he sees it not. You who would make a sacrifice of life, and make your eyes and ears bear witness to the death of God and of His holy Son, think not that you have power to make of Them what God willed not They be. In Heaven, God's Son is not imprisoned in a body, nor is sacrificed in solitude to sin. And as he is in Heaven, so must he be eternally and everywhere. He is the same forever. Born again each instant, untouched by time, and far beyond the reach of any sacrifice of life or death. (T-26.I.7:1-7)

Be innocent of judgment, unaware of any thoughts of evil or of good that ever crossed your mind of anyone. Now do you know him not. But you are free to learn of him, and learn of him anew. Now is he born again to you, and you are born again to him, without the past that sentenced him to die, and you with him. Now is he free to live as you are free, because an ancient learning passed away, and left a place for truth to be reborn. (T-31.I.13:1-5)

> “The lip of truth shall be established for ever: but a lying tongue is but for a moment.” (Proverbs 12:19)

The instant that the mad idea of making your relationship with God unholy seemed to be possible, all your relationships were made meaningless. In that unholy instant time was born, and bodies made to house the mad idea and give it the illusion of reality. And so it seemed to have a home that held together for a little while in time, and vanished. For what could house this mad idea against reality but for an instant? (T-20.VI.8:6-9)

Idols must disappear, and leave no trace behind their going. The unholy instant of their seeming power is frail as is a snowflake, but without its loveliness. Is this the substitute you want for the eternal blessing of the holy instant and its unlimited beneficence? (T-20.VI.9:1-3)

The holy relationship reflects the true relationship the Son of God has with his Father in reality. The Holy Spirit rests within it in the certainty it will endure forever. Its firm foundation is eternally upheld by truth, and love shines on it with the gentle smile and tender blessing it offers to its own. Here the unholy instant is exchanged in gladness for the holy one of safe return. Here is the way to true relationships held gently open, through which you and your brother walk together, leaving the body thankfully behind and resting in the Everlasting Arms. Love’s Arms are open to receive you, and give you peace forever. (T-20.VI.10:1-6)

> “Without descent, having neither beginning of days, nor end of life; but made like unto the Son of God; abideth a priest continually.” (Hebrews 7:3)

There are no beginnings and no endings in God, Whose universe is Himself. Can you exclude yourself from the universe, or from God Who *is* the universe? I and my Father are one with you, for you are part of Us. Do you really believe that part of God can be missing or lost to Him? (T-11.I.2:3-6)

Speak on Judgment

> "Judge not, and ye shall not be judged: condemn not, and ye shall not be condemned: forgive, and ye shall be forgiven." (Luke 6:37)

Judgment is symbolic because beyond perception there is no judgment. When the Bible says "Judge not that ye be not judged," it means that if you judge the reality of others you will be unable to avoid judging your own. (T-3.VI.1:3-4)

The Holy Spirit does not teach you to judge others, because He does not want you to teach error and learn it yourself. He would hardly be consistent if He allowed you to strengthen what you must learn to avoid. In the mind of the thinker, then, He *is* judgmental, but only in order to unify the mind so it can perceive without judgment. (T-6.V.C.2:1-3)

It is surely good advice to tell you not to judge what you do not understand. No one with a personal investment is a reliable witness, for truth to him has become what he wants it to be. If you are unwilling to perceive an appeal for help as what it is, it is because you are unwilling to give help and to receive it. To fail to recognize a call for help is to refuse help. Would you maintain that you do not need it? Yet this is what you are maintaining when you refuse to recognize a brother's appeal, for only by answering his appeal *can* you be helped. Deny him your help and you will not recognize God's Answer to you. The Holy Spirit does not need your help in interpreting motivation, but you do need His. (T-12.I.5:1-8)

When you look within and see me, it will be because you have decided to manifest truth. And as you manifest it you will see it both without and within. You will see it without *because* you saw it first within. Everything you behold without is a judgment of what you beheld within. If it is your judgment it will be wrong, for judgment is not your function. If it is the judgment of the Holy Spirit it will be right, for judgment *is* His function. You share His function only by judging as He does, reserving no judgment at all for yourself. You will judge against yourself, but He will judge *for* you. (T-12.VII.12:1-8)

As you look upon yourself and judge what you do honestly, you may be tempted to wonder how you can be guiltless. Yet consider this: You are not guiltless in time, but in eternity. You have "sinned" in the past, but there is no past. Always has no direction. Time seems to go in one direction, but when you reach its end it will roll up like a long carpet spread along the past behind you, and will disappear. As long as you believe the Son of God is guilty you will walk along this carpet, believing that it leads to death. And the journey will seem long and cruel and senseless, for so it is. (T-13.I.3:1-7)

> "And the whole earth was of one language, and of one speech." (Genesis 11:1)

> "And the LORD said, Behold, the people is one, and they have all one language; and this they begin to do: and now nothing will be restrained from them, which they have imagined to do." (Genesis 11:6)

It is impossible to communicate in alien tongues. You and your Creator can communicate through creation, because that, and only that is Your joint Will. A divided mind cannot communicate, because it speaks for different things to the same mind. This loses the ability to communicate simply because confused communication does not mean anything. A message cannot be communicated unless it makes sense. How sensible can your messages be, when you ask for what you do not want? Yet as long as you are afraid of your will, that is precisely what you are asking for. (T-9.I.6:1-7)

You may insist that the Holy Spirit does not answer you, but it might be wiser to consider the kind of questioner you are. You do not ask only for what you want. This is because you are afraid you might receive it, and you would. That is why you persist in asking the teacher who could not possibly give you what you want. Of him you can never learn what it is, and this gives you the illusion of safety. Yet you cannot be safe *from* truth, but only *in* truth. Reality is the only safety. (T-9.I.7:1-7)

> "And we have known and believed the love that God hath to us. God is love; and he that dwelleth in love dwelleth in God, and God in him." (1 John 4:16)

God is Love and you do want Him. This *is* your will. Ask for this and you will be answered, because you will be asking only for what belongs to you. (T-9.I.9:7-9)

At God's altar Christ waits for the restoration of Himself in you. God knows His Son as wholly blameless as Himself, and He is approached through the appreciation of His Son. Christ waits for your acceptance of Him as yourself, and of His Wholeness as yours. For Christ is the Son of God, Who lives in His Creator and shines with His glory. Christ is the extension of the Love and the loveliness of God, as perfect as His Creator and at peace with Him. (T-11.IV.7:1-5)

Blessed is the Son of God whose radiance is of his Father, and whose glory he wills to share as his Father shares it with him. There is no condemnation in the Son, for there is no condemnation in the Father. Sharing the perfect Love of the Father the Son must share what belongs to Him, for otherwise he will not know the Father or the Son. Peace be unto you who rest in God, and in whom the whole Sonship rests. (T-11.IV.8:1-4)

Speak on Prayer

> "And whatsoever ye shall ask in my name, that will I do, that the Father may be glorified in the Son. If ye shall ask any thing in my name, I will do it." (John 14:13-14)

The Bible enjoins you to be perfect, to heal all errors, to take no thought of the body as separate and to accomplish all things in my name. This is not my name alone, for ours is a shared identification. The Name of God's Son is One, and you are enjoined to do the works of love because we share this Oneness. Our minds are whole because they are one. (T-8.IX.7:1-4)

> "And all things, whatsoever ye shall ask in prayer, believing, ye shall receive." (Matthew 21:22)

> "If ye abide in me, and my words abide in you, ye shall ask what ye will, and it shall be done unto you." (John 15:7)

The Bible emphasizes that all prayer is answered, and this is indeed true. The very fact that the Holy Spirit has been asked for anything will ensure a response. Yet it is equally certain that no response given by Him will ever be one that would increase fear. It is possible that His answer will not be heard. It is impossible, however, that it will be lost. There are many answers you have already received but have not yet heard. I assure you that they are waiting for you. (T-9.II.3:1-7)

> "Ask, and it shall be given you; seek, and ye shall find; knock, and it shall be opened unto you: Every one that asketh receiveth; and he that seeketh findeth; and to him that knocketh it shall be opened." (Matthew 7:7-8)

The Bible gives many references to the immeasurable gifts which are for you, but for which you must ask. This is not a condition as the ego sets conditions. It is the glorious condition of what you are. (T-4.III.5:3-5)

Let us ask the Father in my name to keep you mindful of His Love for you and yours for Him. He has never failed to answer this request, because it asks only for what He has already willed. Those who call truly are always answered. (T-4.III.6:3-5)

"Seek and ye shall find" does not mean that you should seek blindly and desperately for something you would not recognize. Meaningful seeking is consciously undertaken, consciously organized and consciously directed. The goal must be formulated clearly and kept in mind. Learning and wanting to learn are inseparable. You learn best when you believe what you are trying to learn is of value to you. However, not everything you may want to learn has lasting value. Indeed, many of the things you want to learn may be chosen *because* their value will not last. (T-4.V.5:2-8)

Seek ye first the Kingdom of Heaven, because that is where the laws of God operate truly, and they can operate only truly because they are the laws of truth. But seek this only, because you can find nothing else. There *is* nothing else. God is All in all in a very literal sense. All being is in Him Who is all Being. You are therefore in Him since your being is His. Healing is a way of forgetting the sense of danger the ego has induced in you, by not recognizing its existence in your brother. This strengthens the Holy Spirit in both of you, because it is a refusal to acknowledge fear. Love needs only this invitation. It comes freely to all the Sonship, being what the Sonship is. By your awakening to it, you are merely forgetting what you are not. This enables you to remember what you are. (T-7.IV.7:1-12)

Ask and it shall be given you, because it has already *been* given. Ask for light and learn that you *are* light. If you want understanding and enlightenment you will learn it, because your decision to learn it is the decision to listen to the Teacher Who knows of light, and can therefore teach it to you. (T-8.III.1:2-4)

No one can withhold truth except from himself. Yet God will not refuse you the Answer He gave. Ask, then, for what is yours, but which you did not make, and do not defend yourself against truth. You made the problem God has answered. Ask yourself, therefore, but one simple question:

Do I want the problem or do I want the answer?

Decide for the answer and you will have it, for you will see it as it is, and it is yours already. (T-11.VIII.4:1-7)

The ego is certain that love is dangerous, and this is always its central teaching. It never puts it this way; on the contrary, everyone who believes that the ego is salvation seems to be intensely engaged in the search for love. Yet the ego, though encouraging the search for love very actively, makes one proviso; do not find it. Its dictates, then, can be summed up simply as: "Seek and do *not* find." This is the one promise the ego holds out to you, and the one promise it will keep. (T-12.IV.1:1-5)

I am the manifestation of the Holy Spirit, and when you see me it will be because you have invited Him. For He will send you His witnesses if you will but look upon them. Remember always that you see what you seek, for what you seek you will find. The ego finds what it seeks, and only that. It does not find love, for that is not what it is seeking. Yet seeking and finding are the same, and if you seek for two goals you will find them, but you will recognize neither. You will think they are the same because you want both of them. The mind always strives for integration, and if it is split and wants to keep the split, it will still believe it has one goal by making it seem to be one. (T-12.VII.6:1-8)

You will see me as you learn the Son of God is guiltless. He has always sought his guiltlessness, and he has found it. For everyone is seeking to escape from the prison he has made, and the way to find release is not denied him. Being in him, he has found it. *When* he finds it is only a matter of time, and time is but an illusion. For the Son of God is guiltless now, and the brightness of his purity shines untouched forever in God's Mind. God's Son will always be as he was created. (T-13.I.5:1-7)

Prayer is the greatest gift with which God blessed His Son at his creation. It was then what it is to become; the single voice Creator and creation share; the song the Son sings to the Father, Who returns the thanks it offers Him unto the Son. Endless the harmony, and endless, too, the joyous concord of the Love They give forever to Each Other. And in this, creation is extended. God gives thanks to His extension in His Son. His Son gives thanks for his creation, in the song of his creating in his Father's Name. The Love They share is what all prayer will be throughout eternity, when time is done. For such it was before time seemed to be. (S-1.in.1:1-8)

To you who are in time a little while, prayer takes the form that best will suit your need. You have but one. What God created one must recognize its oneness, and rejoice that what illusions seemed to separate is one forever in the Mind of God. Prayer now must be the means by which God's Son leaves separate goals and separate interests by, and turns in holy gladness to the truth of union in his Father and himself. (S-1.in.2:1-4)

Lay down your dreams, you holy Son of God, and rising up as God created you, dispense with idols and remember Him. Prayer will sustain you now, and bless you as you lift your heart to Him in rising song that reaches higher and then higher still, until both high and low have disappeared. Faith in your goal will grow and hold you up as you ascend the shining stairway to the lawns of Heaven and the gate of peace. For this is prayer and here salvation is. This is the way. It is God's gift to you. (S-1.in.3:1-6)

The secret of true prayer is to forget the things you think you need. To ask for the specific is much the same as to look on sin and then forgive it. Also in the same way, in prayer you overlook your specific needs as you see them, and let them go into God's Hands. There they become your gifts to Him, for they tell Him that you would have no gods before Him; no love but His. What could His answer be but your remembrance of Him? Can this be traded for a bit of trifling advice about a problem of an instant's duration? God answers only for eternity. But still all little answers are contained in this. (S-1.I.4:1-8)

> "But seek ye first the kingdom of God, and his righteousness; and all these things shall be added unto you." (Matthew 6:33)

Seek ye first the Kingdom of Heaven, because that is where the laws of God operate truly, and they can operate only truly because they are the laws of truth. But seek this only, because you can find nothing else. There *is* nothing else. (T-7.IV.7:1-3)

Instead of "Seek ye first the Kingdom of Heaven" say, "*Will* ye first the Kingdom of Heaven," and you have said, "I know what I am and I accept my own inheritance." (T-3.VI.11:8)

> "And he spake this parable unto certain which trusted in themselves that they were righteous, and despised others: Two men went up into the temple to pray; the one a Pharisee, and the other a publican.
>
> The Pharisee stood and prayed thus with himself, God, I thank thee, that I am not as other men are, extortioners, unjust,

> adulterers, or even as this publican. I fast twice in the week, I give tithes of all that I possess. And the publican, standing afar off, would not lift up so much as his eyes unto heaven, but smote upon his breast, saying, God be merciful to me a sinner.
>
> I tell you, this man went down to his house justified rather than the other: for every one that exalteth himself shall be abased; and he that humbleth himself shall be exalted." (Luke 18:9-14)

Prayer is a way to true humility. And here again it rises slowly up, and grows in strength and love and holiness. Let it but leave the ground where it begins to rise to God, and true humility will come at last to grace the mind that thought it was alone and stood against the world. Humility brings peace because it does not claim that you must rule the universe, nor judge all things as you would have them be. All little gods it gladly lays aside, not in resentment, but in honesty and recognition that they do not serve. (S-1.V.1:1-5)

Illusions and humility have goals so far apart they cannot coexist, nor share a dwelling place where they can meet. Where one has come the other disappears. The truly humble have no goal but God because they need no idols, and defense no longer serves a purpose. Enemies are useless now, because humility does not oppose. It does not hide in shame because it is content with what it is, knowing creation is the Will of God. Its selflessness is Self, and this it sees in every meeting, where it gladly joins with every Son of God, whose purity it recognizes that it shares with him. (S-1.V.2:1-6)

Now prayer is lifted from the world of things, of bodies, and of gods of every kind, and you can rest in holiness at last. (S-1.V.3:1)

> "God is a Spirit: and they that worship him must worship [him] in spirit and in truth." (John 4:24)
>
> "And when thou prayest, thou shalt not be as the hypocrites are: for they love to pray standing in the synagogues and in the corners of the streets, that they may be seen of men. Verily I say unto you, They have their reward. But thou, when thou prayest, enter into thy closet, and when thou hast shut thy door, pray to thy Father which is in secret; and thy Father which seeth in secret shall reward thee openly.

> But when ye pray, use not vain repetitions, as the heathen do: for they think that they shall be heard for their much speaking. Be not ye therefore like unto them: for your Father knoweth what things ye have need of, before ye ask him." (Matthew 6:5-8)

> "Behold, thou desirest truth in the inward parts: and in the hidden part thou shalt make me to know wisdom." (Psalms 51:6)

Prayer is a stepping aside; a letting go, a quiet time of listening and loving. It should not be confused with supplication of any kind, because it is a way of remembering your holiness. Why should holiness entreat, being fully entitled to everything Love has to offer? And it is to Love you go in prayer. Prayer is an offering; a giving up of yourself to be at one with Love. There is nothing to ask because there is nothing left to want. That nothingness becomes the altar of God. (S-1.I.5:1-7)

Speak on Union and Holy Relationship

> "And the Word was made flesh, and dwelt among us, and we beheld his glory, the glory as of the only begotten of the Father, full of grace and truth." (John 1:14)

The Bible says, "The Word (or thought) was made flesh." Strictly speaking this is impossible, since it seems to involve the translation of one order of reality into another. Different orders of reality merely appear to exist, just as different orders of miracles do. Thought cannot be made into flesh except by belief, since thought is not physical. Yet thought is communication, for which the body can be used. This is the only natural use to which it can be put. To use the body unnaturally is to lose sight of the Holy Spirit's purpose, and thus to confuse the goal of His curriculum. (T-8.VII.7:1-7)

You are not limited by the body, and thought cannot be made flesh. Yet mind can be manifested through the body if it goes beyond it and does not interpret it as limitation. Whenever you see another as limited to or by the body, you are imposing this limit on yourself. Are you willing to accept this, when your whole purpose for learning should be to escape from limitations? To conceive of the body as a means of attack and to believe that joy could possibly result, is a clear-cut indication of a poor learner. He has accepted a learning goal in obvious contradiction to the unified purpose of the curriculum, and one that is interfering with his ability to accept its purpose as his own. (T-8.VII.14:1-6)

> "Honour all men. Love the brotherhood." (1 Peter 2:17)

Everyone on earth has formed special relationships, and although this is not so in Heaven, the Holy Spirit knows how to bring a touch of Heaven to them here. In the holy instant no one is special, for your personal needs intrude on no one to make your brothers seem different. Without the values from the past, you would see them all the same and like yourself. (T-15.V.8:1-3)

Whenever you are angry, you can be sure that you have formed a special relationship which the ego has "blessed," for anger *is* its blessing. (T-15.VII.10:1)

> "For who knoweth what is good for man in this life, all the days of his vain life which he spendeth as a shadow? For who can tell a man what shall be after him under the sun?" (Ecclesiastes 6:12)

It is through these strange and shadowy figures that the insane relate to their insane world. ... Again and again have you attacked your brother, because you saw in him a shadow figure in your private world. And thus it is you must attack yourself first, for what you attack is not in others. (T-13.V.3:1-7)

Your relationship with your brother has been uprooted from the world of shadows, and its unholy purpose has been safely brought through the barriers of guilt, washed with forgiveness, and set shining and firmly rooted in the world of light. From there it calls to you to follow the course it took, lifted high above the darkness and gently placed before the gates of Heaven. The holy instant in which you and your brother were united is but the messenger of love, sent from beyond forgiveness to remind you of all that lies beyond it. Yet it is through forgiveness that it will be remembered. (T-18.IX.13:1-4)

Is it too much to ask a little trust for him who carries Christ to you, that you may be forgiven all your sins, and left without a single one you cherish still? Forget not that a shadow held between your brother and yourself obscures the face of Christ and memory of God. And would you trade Them for an ancient hate? The ground whereon you stand is holy ground because of Them Who, standing there with you, have blessed it with Their innocence and peace. (T-26.IX.2:1-4)

It is impossible to use one relationship at the expense of another and not to suffer guilt. And it is equally impossible to condemn part of a relationship and find peace within it. Under the Holy Spirit's teaching all relationships are seen as total commitments, yet they do not conflict with one another in any way. Perfect faith in each one, for its ability to satisfy you completely, arises only from perfect faith in yourself. (T-15.VI.1:1-4)

Relate only with what will never leave you, and what you can never leave. (T-15.VIII.3:1)

You are forever in a relationship so holy that it calls to everyone to escape from loneliness, and join you in your love. (T-15.VIII.3:8)

For God created the only relationship that has meaning, and that is His relationship with you. (T-15.VIII.6:6)

When the body ceases to attract you, and when you place no value on it as a means of getting anything, then there will be no interference in communication and your thoughts will be as free as God's. ... The reality of this relationship becomes the only truth that you could ever want. All truth *is* here. (T-15.IX.7:1-6)

The holy relationship, a major step toward the perception of the real world, is learned. It is the old, unholy relationship, transformed and seen anew. The holy relationship is a phenomenal teaching accomplishment. In all its aspects, as it begins, develops and becomes accomplished, it represents the reversal of the unholy relationship. (T-17.V.2:1-4)

A holy relationship starts from a different premise. Each one has looked within and seen no lack. Accepting his completion, he would extend it by joining with another, whole as himself. He sees no difference between these selves, for differences are only of the body. Therefore, he looks on nothing he would take. He denies not his own reality *because* it is the truth. Just under Heaven does he stand, but close enough not to return to earth. For this relationship has Heaven's Holiness. How far from home can a relationship so like to Heaven be? (T-22.in.3:1-9)

Think what a holy relationship can teach! Here is belief in differences undone. Here is the faith in differences shifted to sameness. ... Reason now can lead you and your brother to the logical conclusion of your union. It must extend, as you extended when you and he joined. It must reach out beyond itself, as you reached out beyond the body, to let you and your brother be joined. And now the sameness that you saw extends and finally removes all sense of differences, so that the sameness that lies beneath them all becomes apparent. Here is the golden circle where you recognize the Son of God. For what is born into a holy relationship can never end. (T-22.in.4:1-10)

Beyond the body that you interposed between you and your brother, and shining in the golden light that reaches it from the bright, endless circle that extends forever, is your holy relationship, beloved of God Himself. How still it rests, in time and yet beyond, immortal yet on earth. How great the power that lies in it. Time waits upon its will, and earth will be as it would have it be. Here is no separate will, nor the desire that anything be separate. Its will has no exceptions, and what it wills is true. Every illusion brought to its forgiveness is gently overlooked and disappears. For at its center Christ has been reborn, to light His home with vision that overlooks the world. Would you not have this holy home be yours as well? No misery is here, but only joy. (T-22.II.12:1-10)

> "Then Peter opened his mouth, and said, Of a truth I perceive that God is no respecter of persons." (Acts 10:34)

> "He that loveth father or mother more than me is not worthy of me: and he that loveth son or daughter more than me is not worthy of me." (Matthew 10:37)

You cannot enter into real relationships with any of God's Sons unless you love them all and equally. Love is not special. If you single out part of the Sonship for your love, you are imposing guilt on all your relationships and making them unreal. You can love only as God loves. Seek not to love unlike Him, for there is no love apart from His. Until you recognize that this is true, you will have no idea what love is like. (T-13.X.11:1-6)

The Holy Spirit knows no one is special. Yet He also perceives that you have made special relationships, which He would purify and not let you destroy. However unholy the reason you made them may be, He can translate them into holiness by removing as much fear as you will let Him. (T-15.V.5:1-3)

> "What therefore God hath joined together, let not man put asunder." (Matthew 19:6)

Whom God has joined cannot be separated, and God has joined all His Sons with Himself. Can you be separated from your life and your being? (T-8.VI.9:4-5)

Do you want freedom of the body or of the mind? For both you cannot have. Which do you value? Which is your goal? For one you see as means; the other, end. ... No one but yearns for freedom and tries to find it. Yet he will seek for it where he believes it is and can be found. He will believe it possible of mind or body, and he will make the other serve his choice as means to find it. (T-22.VI.1:1-10)

Speak on Lust, Fantasies, and the Desires of the Flesh

"But every man is tempted, when he is drawn away of his own lust, and enticed." (James 1:14)

"For all that is in the world, the lust of the flesh, and the lust of the eyes, and the pride of life, is not of the Father, but is of the world. And the world passeth away, and the lust thereof: but he that doeth the will of God abideth for ever." (1 John 2:16-17)

"I delight to do thy will, O my God: yea, thy law is within my heart." (Psalms 40:8)

Your distorted perceptions produce a dense cover over miracle impulses, making it hard for them to reach your own awareness. The confusion of miracle impulses with physical impulses is a major perceptual distortion. Physical impulses are misdirected miracle impulses. All real pleasure comes from doing God's Will. This is because *not* doing it is a denial of Self. Denial of Self results in illusions, while correction of the error brings release from it. Do not deceive yourself into believing that you can relate in peace to God or to your brothers with anything external. (T-1.VII.1:1-7)

God's teachers can have no regret on giving up the pleasures of the world. Is it a sacrifice to give up pain? Does an adult resent the giving up of children's toys? Does one whose vision has already glimpsed the face of Christ look back with longing on a slaughter house? No one who has escaped the world and all its ills looks back on it with condemnation. Yet he must rejoice that he is free of all the sacrifice its values would demand of him. To them he sacrifices all his peace. To them he sacrifices all his freedom. And to possess them must he sacrifice his hope of Heaven and remembrance of his Father's Love. Who in his sane mind chooses nothing as a substitute for everything? (M-13.4:1-10)

The Holy Spirit does not demand you sacrifice the hope of the body's pleasure; it *has* no hope of pleasure. But neither can it bring you fear of pain. Pain is the only "sacrifice" the Holy Spirit asks, and this He *would* remove. (T-19.IV.B.3:5-7)

It is impossible to seek for pleasure through the body and not find pain. It is essential that this relationship be understood, for it is one the ego sees as proof of sin. It is not really punitive at all. It is but the inevitable result of equating yourself with the body, which is the invitation to pain. For it invites fear to enter and become your purpose. The attraction of guilt *must* enter with it, and whatever fear directs the body to do is therefore painful. It will share the pain of all illusions, and the illusion of pleasure will be the same as pain. (T-19.IV.B.12:1-7)

> "Then said Jesus, Father, forgive them; for they know not what they do." (Luke 23:34)
>
> "Lust not after her beauty in thine heart." (Proverbs 6:25)
>
> "This I say then, Walk in the Spirit, and ye shall not fulfil the lust of the flesh." (Galatians 5:16)
>
> "But I say unto you, That whosoever looketh on a woman to lust after her hath committed adultery with her already in his heart." (Matthew 5:28)

Fantasies of any kind are distortions, because they always involve twisting perception into unreality. Actions that stem from distortions are literally the reactions of those who know not what they do. Fantasy is an attempt to control reality according to false needs. Twist reality in any way and you are perceiving destructively. Fantasies are a means of making false associations and attempting to obtain pleasure from them. But although you can perceive false associations, you can never make them real except to yourself. You believe in what you make. If you offer miracles, you will be equally strong in your belief in them. The strength of your conviction will then sustain the belief of the miracle receiver. (T-1.VII.3:2-10)

The special love relationship is the ego's most boasted gift, and one which has the most appeal to those unwilling to relinquish guilt. The "dynamics" of the ego are clearest here, for counting on the attraction of this offering, the fantasies that center around it are often quite overt. Here they are usually judged to be acceptable and even natural. (T-16.V.3:1-3)

It is not easy to realize that prayers for things, for status, for human love, for external "gifts" of any kind, are always made to set up jailers and to hide from guilt. These things are used for goals that substitute for God, and therefore distort the purpose of prayer. The desire for them *is* the prayer. One need not ask explicitly. The goal of God is lost in the quest for lesser goals of any kind, and prayer becomes requests for enemies. The power of prayer can be quite clearly recognized even in this. No one who wants an enemy will fail to find one. But just as surely will he lose the only true goal that is given him. Think of the cost, and understand it well. All other goals are at the cost of God. (S-1.III.6:1-10)

Speak on Celibacy and Chastity

> "All men cannot receive this saying, save they to whom it is given. For there are some eunuchs, which were so born from their mother's womb: and there are some eunuchs, which were made eunuchs of men: and there be eunuchs, which have made themselves eunuchs for the kingdom of heaven's sake. He that is able to receive it, let him receive it." (Matthew 19:11-12)

The ego uses the body for attack, for pleasure and for pride. The insanity of this perception makes it a fearful one indeed. The Holy Spirit sees the body only as a means of communication, and because communicating is sharing it becomes communion. (T-6.V.A.5:3-5)

In the holy instant, where the Great Rays replace the body in awareness, the recognition of relationships without limits is given you. But in order to see this, it is necessary to give up every use the ego has for the body, and to accept the fact that the ego has no purpose you would share with it. For the ego would limit everyone to a body for its own purposes, and while you think it has a purpose, you will choose to utilize the means by which it tries to turn its purpose into accomplishment. This will never be accomplished. Yet you have surely recognized that the ego, whose goals are altogether unattainable, will strive for them with all its might, and will do so with the strength that you have given it. (T-15.IX.3:1-5)

Communication ends separation. Attack promotes it. The body is beautiful or ugly, peaceful or savage, helpful or harmful, according to the use to which it is put. And in the body of another you will see the use to which you have put yours. If the body becomes a means you give to the Holy Spirit to use on behalf of union of the Sonship, you will not see anything physical except as what it is. Use it for truth and you will see it truly. Misuse it and you will misunderstand it, because you have already done so *by* misusing it. Interpret anything apart from the Holy Spirit and you will mistrust it. This will lead you to hatred and attack and loss of peace. (T-8.VII.4:1-9)

As "something" is the body asked to be God's enemy, replacing what He is with littleness and limit and despair. It is His loss you celebrate when you behold the body as a thing you love, or look upon it as a thing you hate. For if He be the sum of everything, then what is not in Him does not exist, and His completion is its nothingness. (T-29.II.10:1-3)

How Would You Have Me Look upon the Body?

> "What? know ye not that your body is the temple of the Holy Ghost which is in you, which ye have of God, and ye are not your own?" (1 Corinthians 6:19)

The Atonement can only be accepted within you by releasing the inner light. Since the separation, defenses have been used almost entirely to defend *against* the Atonement, and thus maintain the separation. This is generally seen as a need to protect the body. The many body fantasies in which minds engage arise from the distorted belief that the body can be used as a means for attaining "atonement." Perceiving the body as a temple is only the first step in correcting this distortion, because it alters only part of it. It *does* recognize that Atonement in physical terms is impossible. The next step, however, is to realize that a temple is not a structure at all. Its true holiness lies at the inner altar around which the structure is built. The emphasis on beautiful structures is a sign of the fear of Atonement, and an unwillingness to reach the altar itself. The real beauty of the temple cannot be seen with the physical eye. Spiritual sight, on the other hand, cannot see the structure at all because it is perfect vision. It can, however, see the altar with perfect clarity. (T-2.III.1:1-12)

In this world, not even the body is perceived as whole. Its purpose is seen as fragmented into many functions with little or no relationship to each other, so that it appears to be ruled by chaos. Guided by the ego, it *is*. Guided by the Holy Spirit, it is not. It becomes a means by which the part of the mind you tried to separate *from* spirit can reach beyond its distortions and return *to* spirit. The ego's temple thus becomes the temple of the Holy Spirit, where devotion to Him replaces devotion to the ego. In this sense the body does become a temple to God; His Voice abides in it by directing the use to which it is put. (T-8.VII.9:1-7)

The Holy Spirit's temple is not a body, but a relationship. The body is an isolated speck of darkness; a hidden secret room, a tiny spot of senseless mystery, a meaningless enclosure carefully protected, yet hiding nothing. Here the unholy relationship escapes reality, and seeks for crumbs to keep itself alive. Here it would drag its brothers, holding them here in its idolatry. Here it is "safe," for here love cannot enter. The Holy Spirit does not build His temples where love can never be. Would He Who sees the face of Christ choose as His home the only place in all the universe where it can not be seen? (T-20.VI.5:1-7)

Idolaters will always be afraid of love, for nothing so severely threatens them as love's approach. Let love draw near them and overlook the body, as it will surely do, and they retreat in fear, feeling the seeming firm foundation of their temple begin to shake and loosen. Brother, you tremble with them. Yet what you fear is but the herald of escape. This place of darkness is not your home. Your temple is not threatened. You are an idolater no longer. The Holy Spirit's purpose lies safe in your relationship, and not your body. You have escaped the body. Where you are the body cannot enter, for the Holy Spirit has set His temple there. (T-20.VI.7:1-10)

Then lay aside the body and quietly transcend it, rising to welcome what you really want. And from His holy temple, look you not back on what you have awakened from. For no illusions can attract the mind that has transcended them, and left them far behind. (T-20.VI.9:5-7)

> "For he that soweth to his flesh shall of the flesh reap corruption; but he that soweth to the Spirit shall of the Spirit reap life everlasting." (Galatians 6:8)

> "That which is born of the flesh is flesh; and that which is born of the Spirit is spirit." (John 3:6)

You see the flesh or recognize the spirit. There is no compromise between the two. If one is real the other must be false, for what is real denies its opposite. There is no choice in vision but this one. What you decide in this determines all you see and think is real and hold as true. On this one choice does all your world depend, for here have you established what you are, as flesh or spirit in your own belief. If you choose flesh, you never will escape the body as your own reality, for you have chosen that you want it so. But choose the spirit, and all Heaven bends to touch your eyes and bless your holy sight, that you may see the world of flesh no more except to heal and comfort and to bless. (T-31.VI.1:1-8)

Speak on the Deception of Seeking and Holding Idols

"Thou shalt have no other gods before me." (Exodus 20:3)

"Lay not up for yourselves treasures upon earth, where moth and rust doth corrupt, and where thieves break through and steal: But lay up for yourselves treasures in heaven, where neither moth nor rust doth corrupt, and where thieves do not break through nor steal." (Matthew 6:19-20)

No force except your own will is strong enough or worthy enough to guide you. In this you are as free as God, and must remain so forever. Let us ask the Father in my name to keep you mindful of His Love for you and yours for Him. He has never failed to answer this request, because it asks only for what He has already willed. Those who call truly are always answered. Thou shalt have no other gods before Him because there *are* none. (T-4.III.6:1-6)

"Let no man deceive himself. If any man among you seemeth to be wise in this world, let him become a fool, that he may be wise." (1 Corinthians 3:18)

"For thus saith the LORD of hosts, the God of Israel; Let not your prophets and your diviners, that be in the midst of you, deceive you, neither hearken to your dreams which ye cause to be dreamed." (Jeremiah 29:8)

"What profiteth the graven image that the maker thereof hath graven it; the molten image, and a teacher of lies, that the maker of his work trusteth therein, to make dumb idols?" (Habakkuk 2:18)

"Confounded be all they that serve graven images, that boast themselves of idols." (Psalms 97:7)

"A drought is upon her waters; and they shall be dried up: for it is the land of graven images, and they are mad upon their idols." (Jeremiah 50:38)

You are the dreamer of the world of dreams. No other cause it has, nor ever will. Nothing more fearful than an idle dream has terrified God's Son, and made him think that he has lost his innocence, denied his Father, and made war upon himself. So fearful is the dream, so seeming real, he could not waken to reality without the sweat of terror and a scream of mortal fear, unless a gentler dream preceded his awaking, and allowed his calmer mind to welcome, not to fear, the Voice that calls with love to waken him; a gentler dream, in which his suffering was healed and where his brother was his friend. God willed he waken gently and with joy, and gave him means to waken without fear. (T-27.VII.13:1-5)

I am responsible for what I see.
I choose the feelings I experience, and I decide
upon the goal I would achieve.
And everything that seems to happen to me
I ask for, and receive as I have asked.

Deceive yourself no longer that you are helpless in the face of what is done to you. Acknowledge but that you have been mistaken, and all effects of your mistakes will disappear. (T-21.II.2:3-7)

Seek not outside yourself. For it will fail, and you will weep each time an idol falls. Heaven cannot be found where it is not, and there can be no peace excepting there. Each idol that you worship when God calls will never answer in His place. There is no other answer you can substitute, and find the happiness His answer brings. Seek not outside yourself. For all your pain comes simply from a futile search for what you want, insisting where it must be found. What if it is not there? Do you prefer that you be right or happy? Be you glad that you are told where happiness abides, and seek no longer elsewhere. You will fail. But it is given you to know the truth, and not to seek for it outside yourself. (T-29.VII.1:1-12)

The lingering illusion will impel him to seek out a thousand idols, and to seek beyond them for a thousand more. ... This is the purpose every idol has, for this the role that is assigned to it, and this the role that cannot be fulfilled. (T-29.VII.3:1-5)

Seek not outside yourself. The search implies you are not whole within and fear to look upon your devastation, but prefer to seek outside yourself for what you are. (T-29.VII.4:5-6)

All idols of this world were made to keep the truth within from being known to you, and to maintain allegiance to the dream that you must find what is outside yourself to be complete and happy. It is vain to worship idols in the hope of peace. God dwells within, and your completion lies in Him. No idol takes His place. Look not to idols. Do not seek outside yourself. (T-29.VII.6:1-6)

What is an idol? Do you think you know? For idols are unrecognized as such, and never seen for what they really are. That is the only power that they have. Their purpose is obscure, and they are feared and worshipped, both, *because* you do not know what they are for, and why they have been made. An idol is an image of your brother that you would value more than what he is. Idols are made that he may be replaced, no matter what their form. And it is this that never is perceived and recognized. Be it a body or a thing, a place, a situation or a circumstance, an object owned or wanted, or a right demanded or achieved, it is the same. (T-29.VIII.1:1-9)

An idol is a false impression, or a false belief; some form of anti-Christ, that constitutes a gap between the Christ and what you see. An idol is a wish, made tangible and given form, and thus perceived as real and seen outside the mind. Yet it is still a thought, and cannot leave the mind that is its source. Nor is its form apart from the idea it represents. All forms of anti-Christ oppose the Christ. And fall before His face like a dark veil that seems to shut you off from Him, alone in darkness. Yet the light is there. A cloud does not put out the sun. No more a veil can banish what it seems to separate, nor darken by one whit the light itself. (T-29.VIII.3:1-9)

An idol is established by belief, and when it is withdrawn the idol "dies." This is the anti-Christ; the strange idea there is a power past omnipotence, a place beyond the infinite, a time transcending the eternal. Here the world of idols has been set by the idea this power and place and time are given form, and shape the world where the impossible has happened. Here the deathless come to die, the all-encompassing to suffer loss, the timeless to be made the slaves of time. Here does the changeless change; the peace of God, forever given to all living things, give way to chaos. And the Son of God, as perfect, sinless and as loving as his Father, come to hate a little while; to suffer pain and finally to die. (T-29.VIII.6:1-6)

The slave of idols is a willing slave. For willing he must be to let himself bow down in worship to what has no life, and seek for power in the powerless.

What happened to the holy Son of God that this could be his wish; to let himself fall lower than the stones upon the ground, and look to idols that they raise him up? Hear, then, your story in the dream you made, and ask yourself if it be not the truth that you believe that it is not a dream. (T-29.IX.1:1-4)

There is a time when childhood should be passed and gone forever. Seek not to retain the toys of children. Put them all away, for you have need of them no more. The dream of judgment is a children's game, in which the child becomes the father, powerful, but with the little wisdom of a child. (T-29.IX.6:1-4)

The Holy Spirit needs a happy learner, in whom His mission can be happily accomplished. You who are steadfastly devoted to misery must first recognize that you are miserable and not happy. The Holy Spirit cannot teach without this contrast, for you believe that misery *is* happiness. (T-14.II.1:1-3)

How Is Healing Accomplished?

> "But that ye may know that the Son of man hath power on earth to forgive sins, then saith he to the sick of the palsy, Arise, take up thy bed, and go unto thine house." (Matthew 9:6)

> "Jesus turned him about, and when he saw her, he said, Daughter, be of good comfort; thy faith hath made thee whole. And the woman was made whole from that hour." (Matthew 9:22)

When a brother is sick it is because he is not asking for peace, and therefore does not know he has it. The acceptance of peace is the denial of illusion, and sickness *is* an illusion. Yet every Son of God has the power to deny illusions anywhere in the Kingdom, merely by denying them completely in himself. I can heal you because I know you. I know your value for you, and it is this value that makes you whole. A whole mind is not idolatrous, and does not know of conflicting laws. I will heal you merely because I have only one message, and it is true. Your faith in it will make you whole when you have faith in me. (T-10.III.7:1-8)

> "And Jesus went about all Galilee, teaching in their synagogues, and preaching the gospel of the kingdom, and healing all manner of sickness and all manner of disease among the people." (Matthew 4:23)

Healing involves an understanding of what the illusion of sickness is for. Healing is impossible without this. (M-5.1:1-2)

Healing is accomplished the instant the sufferer no longer sees any value in pain. Who would choose suffering unless he thought it brought him something, and something of value to him? (M-5.I.1:1-2)

Healing must occur in exact proportion to which the valuelessness of sickness is recognized. One need but say, "There is no gain at all to me in this" and he is healed. But to say this, one first must recognize certain facts. First, it is obvious that decisions are of the mind, not of the body. If sickness is but a faulty problem-solving approach, it is a decision. And if it is a decision, it is the mind and not the body that makes it. The resistance to recognizing this is enormous, because the existence of the world as you perceive it depends on the body being the decision maker. Terms like "instincts," "reflexes" and the like represent attempts to endow the body with non-mental motivators. Actually, such terms merely state or describe the problem. They do not answer it. (M-5.II.1:1-10)

The acceptance of sickness as a decision of the mind, for a purpose for which it would use the body, is the basis of healing. And this is so for healing in all forms. A patient decides that this is so, and he recovers. If he decides against recovery, he will not be healed. Who is the physician? Only the mind of the patient himself. The outcome is what he decides that it is. Special agents seem to be ministering to him, yet they but give form to his own choice. He chooses them in order to bring tangible form to his desires. And it is this they do, and nothing else. They are not actually needed at all. The patient could merely rise up without their aid and say, "I have no use for this." There is no form of sickness that would not be cured at once. (M-5.II.2:1-13)

What is the single requisite for this shift in perception? It is simply this; the recognition that sickness is of the mind, and has nothing to do with the body. What does this recognition "cost"? It costs the whole world you see, for the world will never again appear to rule the mind. For with this recognition is responsibility placed where it belongs; not with the world, but on him who looks on the world and sees it as it is not. He looks on what he chooses to see. No more and no less. The world does nothing to him. He only thought it did. Nor does he do anything to the world, because he was mistaken about what it is. Herein is the release from guilt and sickness both, for they are one. Yet to accept this release, the insignificance of the body must be an acceptable idea. (M-5.II.3:1-12)

With this idea is pain forever gone. But with this idea goes also all confusion about creation. Does not this follow of necessity? Place cause and effect in their true sequence in one respect, and the learning will generalize and transform the world. The transfer value of one true idea has no end or limit. The final outcome of this lesson is the remembrance of God. What do guilt and sickness, pain, disaster and all suffering mean now? Having no purpose, they are gone. And with them also go all the effects they seemed to cause. Cause and effect but replicate creation. Seen in their proper perspective, without distortion and without fear, they re-establish Heaven. (M-5.II.4:1-11)

> "Not every one that saith unto me, Lord, Lord, shall enter into the kingdom of heaven; but he that doeth the will of my Father which is in heaven." (Matthew 7:21)

Strictly speaking, words play no part at all in healing. The motivating factor is prayer, or asking. What you ask for you receive. But this refers to the prayer of the heart, not to the words you use in praying. Sometimes the words and the prayer are contradictory; sometimes they agree. It does not matter. God does not understand words, for they were made by separated minds to keep them in the illusion of separation. Words can be helpful, particularly for the beginner, in helping concentration and facilitating the exclusion, or at least the control, of extraneous thoughts. (M-21.1:1-8)

> "For the LORD giveth wisdom: out of his mouth cometh knowledge and understanding." (Proverbs 2:6)

> "For this cause we also, since the day we heard it, do not cease to pray for you, and to desire that ye might be filled with the knowledge of his will in all wisdom and spiritual understanding." (Colossians 1:9)

> "Happy is the man that findeth wisdom, and the man that getteth understanding." (Proverbs 3:13)

> "To know wisdom and instruction; to perceive the words of understanding; To receive the instruction of wisdom, justice, and judgment, and equity; To give subtlety to the simple, to the young man knowledge and discretion. A wise man will hear, and will increase learning; and a man of understanding shall attain unto wise counsels." (Proverbs 1:2-5)

> "Behold, happy is the man whom God correcteth: therefore despise not thou the chastening of the Almighty." (Job 5:17)

Correct and learn, and be open to learning. You have not made truth, but truth can still set you free. Look as the Holy Spirit looks, and understand as He understands. (T-5.III.11:4-6)

You have been asked to take me as your model for learning, since an extreme example is a particularly helpful learning device. (T-6.in.2:1)

Come therefore unto me, and learn of the truth in you. The mind we share is shared by all our brothers, and as we see them truly they will be healed. (T-7.V.11:1-2)

You who are beloved of God are wholly blessed. Learn this of me, and free the holy will of all those who are as blessed as you are. (T-8.VI.10:4-5)

God's Son *is* saved. Bring only this awareness to the Sonship, and you will have a part in the redemption as valuable as mine. For your part must be like mine if you learn it of me. (T-11.VI.10:1-3)

Why would you struggle so frantically to anticipate all you cannot know, when all knowledge lies behind every decision the Holy Spirit makes for you? Learn of His wisdom and His Love, and teach His answer to everyone who struggles in the dark. For you decide for them and for yourself. (T-14.III.16:3-5)

Holy child of God, when will you learn that only holiness can content you and give you peace? Remember that you learn not for yourself alone, no more than I did. It is because I learned for you that you can learn of me. (T-15.III.9:1-3)

Speak on Trying to Serve Two Masters

> "No man can serve two masters: for either he will hate the one, and love the other; or else he will hold to the one, and despise the other." (Matthew 6:24)

Whatever is true is eternal, and cannot change or be changed. Spirit is therefore unalterable because it is already perfect, but the mind can elect what it chooses to serve. The only limit put on its choice is that it cannot serve two masters. If it elects to do so, the mind can become the medium by which spirit creates along the line of its own creation. If it does not freely elect to do so, it retains its creative potential but places itself under tyrannous rather than Authoritative control. As a result it imprisons, because such are the dictates of tyrants. (T-1.V.5:1-6)

> "For he that wavereth is like a wave of the sea driven with the wind and tossed. For let not that man think that he shall receive any thing of the Lord. A double minded man is unstable in all his ways." (James 1:6-8)

> "And Jesus knew their thoughts, and said unto them, Every kingdom divided against itself is brought to desolation; and every city or house divided against itself shall not stand." (Matthew 12:25)

How can the resting place of God turn on itself, and seek to overcome the One Who dwells there? And think what happens when the house of God perceives itself divided. The altar disappears, the light grows dim, the temple of the Holy One becomes a house of sin. And nothing is remembered except illusions. Illusions can conflict, because their forms are different. And they do battle only to establish which form is true. (T-23.I.11:1-6)

You are not called upon to do what one divided still against himself would find impossible. Have little faith that wisdom could be found in such a state of mind. But be you thankful that only little faith is asked of you. (T-25.VIII.2:5-7)

What Does It Mean to Discern between Real and Unreal?

> "For I know the thoughts that I think toward you, saith the LORD, thoughts of peace, and not of evil, to give you an expected end." (Jeremiah 29:11)

Whatever you accept into your mind has reality for you. It is your acceptance of it that makes it real. If you enthrone the ego in your mind, your allowing it to enter makes it your reality. This is because the mind is capable of creating reality or making illusions. I said before that you must learn to think with God. To think with Him is to think like Him. This engenders joy, not guilt, because it is natural. Guilt is a sure sign that your thinking is unnatural. Unnatural thinking will always be attended with guilt, because it is the belief in sin. (T-5.V.4:1-9)

The thoughts of which I am aware do not mean anything because I am trying to think without God. What I call "my" thoughts are not my real thoughts. My real thoughts are the thoughts I think with God. I am not aware of them because I have made my thoughts to take their place. I am willing to recognize that my thoughts do not mean anything, and to let them go. I choose to have them be replaced by what they were intended to replace. My thoughts are meaningless, but all creation lies in the thoughts I think with God. (W-51.4:2-8)

My mind holds only what I think with God. That is a fact, and represents the truth of What you are and What your Father is. It is this thought by which the Father gave creation to the Son, establishing the Son as co-creator with Himself. It is this thought that fully guarantees salvation to the Son. For in his mind no thoughts can dwell but those his Father shares. Lack of forgiveness blocks this thought from his awareness. Yet it is forever true. (W-rIV.in.2:2-8)

Your self-deceptions cannot take the place of truth. No more than can a child who throws a stick into the ocean change the coming and the going of the tides, the warming of the water by the sun, the silver of the moon on it by night. (W-rIV.in.4:2-3)

Do All My Distortions Arise from My Attack Thoughts?

> "And he saith unto them, Are ye so without understanding also? Do ye not perceive, that whatsoever thing from without entereth into the man, it cannot defile him; Because it entereth not into his heart, but into the belly, and goeth out into the draught, purging all meats? And he said, That which cometh out of the man, that defileth the man. For from within, out of the heart of men, proceed evil thoughts, adulteries, fornications, murders, Thefts, covetousness, wickedness, deceit, lasciviousness, an evil eye, blasphemy, pride, foolishness: All these evil things come from within, and defile the man." (Mark 7:18-23)

I can escape from the world I see by giving up attack thoughts. (W-23)

The idea for today contains the only way out of fear that will ever succeed. Nothing else will work; everything else is meaningless. But this way cannot fail. Every thought you have makes up some segment of the world you see. It is with your thoughts, then, that we must work, if your perception of the world is to be changed. (W-23.1:1-5)

If the cause of the world you see is attack thoughts, you must learn that it is these thoughts which you do not want. There is no point in lamenting the world. There is no point in trying to change the world. It is incapable of change because it is merely an effect. But there is indeed a point in changing your thoughts about the world. Here you are changing the cause. The effect will change automatically. (W-23.2:1-7)

The world you see is a vengeful world, and everything in it is a symbol of vengeance. Each of your perceptions of "external reality" is a pictorial representation of your own attack thoughts. One can well ask if this can be called seeing. Is not fantasy a better word for such a process, and hallucination a more appropriate term for the result? (W-23.3:1-4)

You see the world that you have made, but you do not see yourself as the image maker. You cannot be saved from the world, but you can escape from its cause. This is what salvation means, for where is the world you see when its cause is gone? Vision already holds a replacement for everything you think you see now. Loveliness can light your images, and so transform them that you will love them, even though they were made of hate. For you will not be making them alone. (W-23.4:1-6)

The idea for today introduces the thought that you are not trapped in the world you see, because its cause can be changed. This change requires, first, that the cause be identified and then let go, so that it can be replaced. The first two steps in this process require your cooperation. The final one does not. Your images have already been replaced. By taking the first two steps, you will see that this is so. (W-23.5:1-6)

What Do All the "Watch" Parables Mean?

"Then shall the kingdom of heaven be likened unto ten virgins, which took their lamps, and went forth to meet the bridegroom. And five of them were wise, and five were foolish. They that were foolish took their lamps, and took no oil with them: But the wise took oil in their vessels with their lamps. While the bridegroom tarried, they all slumbered and slept. And at midnight there was a cry made, Behold, the bridegroom cometh; go ye out to meet him. Then all those virgins arose, and trimmed their lamps. And the foolish said unto the wise, Give us of your oil; for our lamps are gone out. But the wise answered, saying, Not so; lest there be not enough for us and you: but go ye rather to them that sell, and buy for yourselves. And while they went to buy, the bridegroom came; and they that were ready went in with him to the marriage: and the door was shut. Afterward came also the other virgins, saying, Lord, Lord, open to us. But he answered and said, Verily I say unto you, I know you not. Watch therefore, for ye know neither the day nor the hour wherein the Son of man cometh." (Matthew 25:1-13)

"For the Son of man is as a man taking a far journey, who left his house, and gave authority to his servants, and to every man his work, and commanded the porter to watch. Watch ye therefore: for ye know not when the master of the house cometh, at even, or at midnight, or at the cockcrowing, or in the morning: Lest coming suddenly he find you sleeping. And what I say unto you I say unto all, Watch." (Mark 13:34-37)

"Let your loins be girded about, and your lights burning; And ye yourselves like unto men that wait for their lord, when he will return from the wedding; that when he cometh and knocketh, they may open unto him immediately. Blessed are those servants, whom the lord when he cometh shall find watching: verily I say unto you, that he shall gird himself, and make them to sit down to meat, and will come forth and serve them. And if he shall come in the second watch, or come in the third watch, and find them

> so, blessed are those servants. And this know, that if the goodman of the house had known what hour the thief would come, he would have watched, and not have suffered his house to be broken through. Be ye therefore ready also: for the Son of man cometh at an hour when ye think not." (Luke 12:35-40)

It has never really entered your mind to give up every idea you ever had that opposes knowledge. You retain thousands of little scraps of fear that prevent the Holy One from entering. Light cannot penetrate through the walls you make to block it, and it is forever unwilling to destroy what you have made. No one can see through a wall, but I can step around it. Watch your mind for the scraps of fear, or you will be unable to ask me to do so. (T-4.III.7:1-5)

Watch carefully and see what it is you are really asking for. Be very honest with yourself in this, for we must hide nothing from each other. If you will really try to do this, you have taken the first step toward preparing your mind for the Holy One to enter. We will prepare for this together, for once He has come, you will be ready to help me make other minds ready for Him. How long will you deny Him His Kingdom? (T-4.III.8:1-5)

Watch your mind for the temptations of the ego, and do not be deceived by it. It offers you nothing. When you have given up this voluntary dis-spiriting, you will see how your mind can focus and rise above fatigue and heal. Yet you are not sufficiently vigilant against the demands of the ego to disengage yourself. *This need not be.* (T-4.IV.6:1-5)

Watch your mind carefully for any beliefs that hinder its accomplishment, and step away from them. Judge how well you have done this by your own feelings, for this is the one right use of judgment. Judgment, like any other defense, can be used to attack or protect; to hurt or to heal. The ego *should* be brought to judgment and found wanting there. Without your own allegiance, protection and love, the ego cannot exist. Let it be judged truly and you must withdraw allegiance, protection and love from it. (T-4.IV.8:5-10)

As you survey your inner world, merely let whatever thoughts cross your mind come into your awareness, each to be considered for a moment, and then replaced by the next. Try not to establish any kind of hierarchy among them. Watch them come and go as dispassionately as possible. Do not dwell on any one in particular, but try to let the stream move on evenly and calmly, without any special investment on your part. (W-31.3:1-4)

Watch the images your imagination presents to your awareness. (W-32.3:4)

Search your mind for fear thoughts, anxiety-provoking situations, "offending" personalities or events, or anything else about which you are harboring unloving thoughts. Note them all casually, repeating the idea for today slowly as you watch them arise in your mind, and let each one go, to be replaced by the next. (W-34.3:2-3)

Watch your mind carefully to catch whatever thoughts cross it. ... Note each one as it comes to you, with as little involvement or concern as possible, dismissing each one by telling yourself:

This thought reflects a goal that is preventing me from accepting my only function. (W-65.5:2-6)

Watch your mind and see, although your eyes are closed, the senseless world you think is real. Review the thoughts as well which are compatible with such a world, and which you think are true. Then let them go, and sink below them to the holy place where they can enter not. There is a door beneath them in your mind, which you could not completely lock to hide what lies beyond. (W-131.11:5-8)

Seek for that door and find it. But before you try to open it, remind yourself no one can fail who seeks to reach the truth. (W-131.12:1-2)

And then we watch our thoughts, appealing silently to Him Who sees the elements of truth in them. Let Him evaluate each thought that comes to mind, remove the elements of dreams, and give them back again as clean ideas that do not contradict the Will of God. (W-151.13:3-4)

Give Him your thoughts, and He will give them back as miracles which joyously proclaim the wholeness and the happiness God wills His Son, as proof of His eternal Love. And as each thought is thus transformed, it takes on healing power from the Mind which saw the truth in it, and failed to be deceived by what was falsely added. All the threads of fantasy are gone. And what remains is unified into a perfect Thought that offers its perfection everywhere. (W-151.14:1-4)

Realize that your forgiveness entitles you to vision. Understand that the Holy Spirit never fails to give the gift of sight to the forgiving. Believe He will not fail you now. You have forgiven the world. He will be with you as you watch and wait. He will show you what true vision sees. It is His Will, and you have joined with Him. Wait patiently for Him. He will be there. (W-75.7:1-9)

Then close your eyes upon the world you see, and in the silent darkness watch the lights that are not of this world light one by one, until where one begins another ends loses all meaning as they blend in one. (W-129.7:5)

Watch with me, angels, watch with me today. Let all God's holy Thoughts surround me, and be still with me while Heaven's Son is born. Let earthly sounds be quiet, and the sights to which I am accustomed disappear. Let Christ be welcomed where He is at home. And let Him hear the sounds He understands, and see but sights that show His Father's Love. Let Him no longer be a stranger here, for He is born again in me today. (W-303.1:1-6)

Today the lights of Heaven bend to you, to shine upon your eyelids as you rest beyond the world of darkness. Here is light your eyes can not behold. And yet your mind can see it plainly, and can understand. A day of grace is given you today, and we give thanks. (W-129.8:1-4)

Awareness of dreaming is the real function of God's teachers. They watch the dream figures come and go, shift and change, suffer and die. Yet they are not deceived by what they see. They recognize that to behold a dream figure as sick and separate is no more real than to regard it as healthy and beautiful. Unity alone is not a thing of dreams. And it is this God's teachers acknowledge as behind the dream, beyond all seeming and yet surely theirs. (M-12.6:6-11)

> "Then shall ye return, and discern between the righteous and the wicked, between him that serveth God and him that serveth him not." (Malachi 3:18)

Nothing the world believes is true. It is a place whose purpose is to be a home where those who claim they do not know themselves can come to question what it is they are. And they will come again until the time Atonement is accepted, and they learn it is impossible to doubt yourself, and not to be aware of what you are. (W-139.7:1-3)

Call all your brothers to witness to his wholeness, as I am calling you to join with me. (T-13.VI.8:6)

Here He leans down to lift you up to Him, out of illusions into holiness; out of the world and to eternity; out of all fear and given back to love. (C-4.8:3)

Your Kingdom is not of this world because it was given you from beyond this world. (T-3.VII.6:9)

Distinguish between Our Father's Law of Love and the Make-Believe Laws of the Ego

> "Think not that I am come to destroy the law, or the prophets: I am not come to destroy, but to fulfill." (Matthew 5:17)

I came to fulfill the law by reinterpreting it. The law itself, if properly understood, offers only protection. (T-1.IV.4:3-4)

> "Let every soul be subject unto the higher powers. For there is no power but of God: the powers that be are ordained of God." (Romans 13:1)

We have observed before how many senseless things have seemed to you to be salvation. Each has imprisoned you with laws as senseless as itself. You are not bound by them. Yet to understand that this is so, you must first realize salvation lies not there. While you would seek for it in things that have no meaning, you bind yourself to laws that make no sense. Thus do you seek to prove salvation is where it is not. (W-76.1:1-6)

Today we will be glad you cannot prove it. For if you could, you would forever seek salvation where it is not, and never find it. The idea for today tells you once again how simple is salvation. Look for it where it waits for you, and there it will be found. Look nowhere else, for it is nowhere else. (W-76.2:1-5)

Think of the freedom in the recognition that you are not bound by all the strange and twisted laws you have set up to save you. ... You really think a small round pellet or some fluid pushed into your veins through a sharpened needle will ward off disease and death. You really think you are alone unless another body is with you. (W-76.3:1-4)

It is insanity that thinks these things. You call them laws, and put them under different names in a long catalogue of rituals that have no use and serve no purpose. You think you must obey the "laws" of medicine, of economics and of health. Protect the body, and you will be saved. (W-76.4:1-4)

These are not laws, but madness. (W-76.5:1)

There are no laws except the laws of God. This needs repeating, over and over, until you realize it applies to everything that you have made in opposition to God's Will. Your magic has no meaning. What it is meant to save does not exist. Only what it is meant to hide will save you. (W-76.6:1-5)

The laws of God can never be replaced. We will devote today to rejoicing that this is so. It is no longer a truth that we would hide. We realize instead it is a truth that keeps us free forever. Magic imprisons, but the laws of God make free. The light has come because there are no laws but His. (W-76.7:1-6)

There are no laws but God's. Dismiss all foolish magical beliefs today, and hold your mind in silent readiness to hear the Voice that speaks the truth to you. You will be listening to One Who says there is no loss under the laws of God. Payment is neither given nor received. Exchange cannot be made; there are no substitutes; and nothing is replaced by something else. God's laws forever give and never take. (W-76.9:1-6)

Hear Him Who tells you this, and realize how foolish are the "laws" you thought upheld the world you thought you saw. Then listen further. He will tell you more. About the Love your Father has for you. About the endless joy He offers you. About His yearning for His only Son, created as His channel for creation; denied to Him by his belief in hell. (W-76.10:1-6)

Let us today open God's channels to Him, and let His Will extend through us to Him. Thus is creation endlessly increased. His Voice will speak of this to us, as well as of the joys of Heaven which His laws keep limitless forever. (W-76.11:1-3)

I am sustained by the Love of God. (W-50)

Here is the answer to every problem that will confront you, today and tomorrow and throughout time. In this world, you believe you are sustained by everything but God. Your faith is placed in the most trivial and insane symbols; pills, money, "protective" clothing, influence, prestige, being liked, knowing the "right" people, and an endless list of forms of nothingness that you endow with magical powers. (W-50.1:1-3)

All these things are your replacements for the Love of God. All these things are cherished to ensure a body identification. They are songs of praise to the ego. Do not put your faith in the worthless. It will not sustain you. (W-50.2:1-5)

Only the Love of God will protect you in all circumstances. It will lift you out of every trial, and raise you high above all the perceived dangers of this world into a climate of perfect peace and safety. It will transport you into a state of mind that nothing can threaten, nothing can disturb, and where nothing can intrude upon the eternal calm of the Son of God. (W-50.3:1-3)

Put not your faith in illusions. They will fail you. Put all your faith in the Love of God within you; eternal, changeless and forever unfailing. This is the answer to whatever confronts you today. Through the Love of God within you, you can resolve all seeming difficulties without effort and in sure confidence. Tell yourself this often today. It is a declaration of release from the belief in idols. It is your acknowledgment of the truth about yourself. (W-50.4:1-8)

Speak on the Topics of Money and Possessions?

> "And he spake a parable unto them, saying, The ground of a certain rich man brought forth plentifully: And he thought within himself, saying, What shall I do, because I have no room where to bestow my fruits? And he said, This will I do: I will pull down my barns, and build greater; and there will I bestow all my fruits and my goods. And I will say to my soul, Soul, thou hast much goods laid up for many years; take thine ease, eat, drink, and be merry. But God said unto him, Thou fool, this night thy soul shall be required of thee: then whose shall those things be, which thou hast provided? So is he that layeth up treasure for himself, and is not rich toward God." (Luke 12:16-21)

> "For the sun is no sooner risen with a burning heat, but it withereth the grass, and the flower thereof falleth, and the grace of the fashion of it perisheth: so also shall the rich man fade away in his ways." (James 1:11)

> "Jesus said unto him, If thou wilt be perfect, go and sell that thou hast, and give to the poor, and thou shalt have treasure in heaven: and come and follow me. But when the young man heard that saying, he went away sorrowful: for he had great possessions. Then said Jesus unto his disciples, Verily I say unto you, That a rich man shall hardly enter into the kingdom of heaven. And again I say unto you, It is easier for a camel to go through the eye of a needle, than for a rich man to enter into the kingdom of God." (Matthew 19:21-24)

I once asked you to sell all you have and give to the poor and follow me. This is what I meant: If you have no investment in anything in this world, you can teach the poor where their treasure is. The poor are merely those who have invested wrongly, and they are poor indeed! Because they are in need it is given you to help them, since you are among them. Consider how perfectly your lesson would be learned if you were unwilling to share their poverty. For poverty is lack, and there is but one lack since there is but one need. (T-12.III.1:1-6)

The world you see holds nothing that you need to offer you; nothing that you can use in any way, nor anything at all that serves to give you joy. Believe this thought, and you are saved from years of misery, from countless disappointments, and from hopes that turn to bitter ashes of despair. No one but must accept this thought as true, if he would leave the world behind and soar beyond its petty scope and little ways. (W-128.1:1-3)

Each thing you value here is but a chain that binds you to the world, and it will serve no other end but this. For everything must serve the purpose you have given it, until you see a different purpose there. The only purpose worthy of your mind this world contains is that you pass it by, without delaying to perceive some hope where there is none. Be you deceived no more. The world you see holds nothing that you want. (W-128.2:1-5)

Escape today the chains you place upon your mind when you perceive salvation here. For what you value you make part of you as you perceive yourself. All things you seek to make your value greater in your sight limit you further, hide your worth from you, and add another bar across the door that leads to true awareness of your Self. (W-128.3:1-3)

> "Lay not up for yourselves treasures upon earth, where moth and rust doth corrupt, and where thieves break through and steal: But lay up for yourselves treasures in heaven, where neither moth nor rust doth corrupt, and where thieves do not break through nor steal: For where your treasure is, there will your heart be also." (Matthew 6:19-21)

> "Again, the kingdom of heaven is like unto treasure hid in a field; the which when a man hath found, he hideth, and for joy thereof goeth and selleth all that he hath, and buyeth that field. Again, the kingdom of heaven is like unto a merchant man, seeking goodly pearls: Lo, when he had found one pearl of great price, went and sold all that he had, and bought it." (Matthew 13:44-46)

What God has willed for you *is* yours. He has given His Will to His treasure, whose treasure it is. Your heart lies where your treasure is, as His does. You who are beloved of God are wholly blessed. Learn this of me, and free the holy will of all those who are as blessed as you are. (T-8.VI.10:1-5)

Behold the Guide your Father gave you, that you might learn you have eternal life. For death is not your Father's Will nor yours, and whatever is true is the Will of the Father. You pay no price for life for that was given you, but you do pay a price for death, and a very heavy one. If death is your treasure, you will sell everything else to purchase it. And you will believe that you have purchased it, because you have sold everything else. Yet you cannot sell the Kingdom of Heaven. Your inheritance can neither be bought nor sold. There can be no disinherited parts of the Sonship, for God is whole and all His extensions are like Him. (T-12.IV.6:1-8)

"For the love of money is the root of all evil." (1 Timothy 6:10)

God is very quiet, for there is no conflict in Him. Conflict is the root of all evil, for being blind it does not see whom it attacks. (T-11.III.1:6-7)

Money is not evil. It is nothing. (P-3.III.1:5-6)

Yet there is a difference between payment and cost. To give money where God's plan allots it has no cost. (P-3.III.2:6-7)

The ego wants to have things for salvation, for possession is its law. Possession for its own sake is the ego's fundamental creed, a basic cornerstone in the churches it builds to itself. And at its altar it demands you lay all of the things it bids you get, leaving you no joy in them. (T-13.VII.10:11-13)

The dreaming of the world takes many forms, because the body seeks in many ways to prove it is autonomous and real. It puts things on itself that it has bought with little metal discs or paper strips the world proclaims as valuable and real. It works to get them, doing senseless things, and tosses them away for senseless things it does not need and does not even want. (T-27.VIII.2:1-3)

There is no sacrifice in the world's terms that does not involve the body. Think a while about what the world calls sacrifice. Power, fame, money, physical pleasure; who is the "hero" to whom all these things belong? Could they mean anything except to a body? Yet a body cannot evaluate. By seeking after such things the mind associates itself with the body, obscuring its Identity and losing sight of what it really is. (M-13.2:4-9)

The Atonement is not the price of your wholeness, but it *is* the price of your awareness of your wholeness. For what you chose to “sell” had to be kept for you, since you could not “buy” it back. Yet you must invest in it, not with money but with spirit. For spirit is will, and will is the “price” of the Kingdom. (T-12.IV.7:1-4)

What Thought Need I Give to My Earthly Needs?

> "Therefore I say unto you, Take no thought for your life, what ye shall eat, or what ye shall drink; nor yet for your body, what ye shall put on. Is not the life more than meat, and the body than raiment? Behold the fowls of the air: for they sow not, neither do they reap, nor gather into barns; yet your heavenly Father feedeth them. Are ye not much better than they? Which of you by taking thought can add one cubit unto his stature? And why take ye thought for raiment? Consider the lilies of the field, how they grow; they toil not, neither do they spin: And yet I say unto you, That even Solomon in all his glory was not arrayed like one of these. Wherefore, if God so clothe the grass of the field, which today is, and to morrow is cast into the oven, shall he not much more clothe you, O ye of little faith? Therefore take no thought, saying, What shall we eat? or, What shall we drink? or, Wherewithal shall we be clothed?" (Matthew 6:25-31)

> "But seek ye first the kingdom of God, and his righteousness; and all these things shall be added unto you." (Matthew 6:33)

Praise, then, the Father for the perfect sanity of His most holy Son. Your Father knoweth that you have need of nothing. In Heaven this is so, for what could you need in eternity? In your world you do need things. It is a world of scarcity in which you find yourself *because* you are lacking. Yet can you find yourself in such a world? Without the Holy Spirit the answer would be no. Yet because of Him the answer is a joyous *yes!* As Mediator between the two worlds, He knows what you have need of and what will not hurt you. (T-13.VII.10:1-9)

Only the Holy Spirit knows what you need. For He will give you all things that do not block the way to light. And what else could you need? In time, He gives you all the things that you need have, and will renew them as long as you have need of them. (T-13.VII.12:1-4)

Once you accept His plan as the one function that you would fulfill, there will be nothing else the Holy Spirit will not arrange for you without your effort. He will go before you making straight your path, and leaving in your way no stones to trip on, and no obstacles to bar your way. Nothing you need will be denied you. Not one seeming difficulty but will melt away before you reach it. You need take thought for nothing, careless of everything except the only purpose that you would fulfill. As that was given you, so will its fulfillment be. God's guarantee will hold against all obstacles, for it rests on certainty and not contingency. It rests on *you.* And what can be more certain than a Son of God? (T-20.IV.8:4-12)

Are There Plans I Need Make to Follow You?

> "Take therefore no thought for the morrow: for the morrow shall take thought for the things of itself." (Matthew 6:34)

> "And as ye go, preach, saying, The kingdom of heaven is at hand. Heal the sick, cleanse the lepers, raise the dead, cast out devils: freely ye have received, freely give. Provide neither gold, nor silver, nor brass in your purses, Nor scrip for your journey, neither two coats, neither shoes, nor yet staves: for the workman is worthy of his meat. And into whatsoever city or town ye shall enter, inquire who in it is worthy; and there abide till ye go thence." (Matthew 10:7-11)

A healed mind does not plan. It carries out the plans that it receives through listening to wisdom that is not its own. It waits until it has been taught what should be done, and then proceeds to do it. It does not depend upon itself for anything except its adequacy to fulfill the plans assigned to it. It is secure in certainty that obstacles can not impede its progress to accomplishment of any goal that serves the greater plan established for the good of everyone. (W-135.11:1-5)

The mind engaged in planning for itself is occupied in setting up control of future happenings. It does not think that it will be provided for, unless it makes its own provisions. Time becomes a future emphasis, to be controlled by learning and experience obtained from past events and previous beliefs. It overlooks the present, for it rests on the idea the past has taught enough to let the mind direct its future course. (W-135.15:1-4)

The mind that plans is thus refusing to allow for change. What it has learned before becomes the basis for its future goals. Its past experience directs its choice of what will happen. And it does not see that here and now is everything it needs to guarantee a future quite unlike the past, without a continuity of any old ideas and sick beliefs. Anticipation plays no part at all, for present confidence directs the way. (W-135.16:1-5)

> "Humble yourselves therefore under the mighty hand of God, that he may exalt you in due time: Casting all your care upon him; for he careth for you." (1 Peter 5:6-7)

Do you really believe you can make a voice that can drown out God's? Do you really believe you can devise a thought system that can separate you from Him? Do you really believe you can plan for your safety and joy better than He can? You need be neither careful nor careless; you need merely cast your cares upon Him because He careth for you. You are His care because He loves you. His Voice reminds you always that all hope is yours because of His care. You cannot choose to escape His care because that is not His Will, but you can choose to accept His care and use the infinite power of His care for all those He created by it. (T-5.VII.1:1-7)

> "Behold, I send you forth as sheep in the midst of wolves: be ye therefore wise as serpents, and harmless as doves." (Matthew 10:16)

God is praised whenever any mind learns to be wholly helpful. This is impossible without being wholly harmless, because the two beliefs must coexist. The truly helpful are invulnerable, because they are not protecting their egos and so nothing can hurt them. (T-4.VII.8:1-3)

The only safety lies in extending the Holy Spirit, because as you see His gentleness in others your own mind perceives itself as totally harmless. Once it can accept this fully, it sees no need to protect itself. The protection of God then dawns upon it, assuring it that it is perfectly safe forever. The perfectly safe are wholly benign. They bless because they know that they are blessed. Without anxiety the mind is wholly kind, and because it extends beneficence it is beneficent. Safety is the complete relinquishment of attack. No compromise is possible in this. (T-6.III.3:1-8)

Christ is reborn as but a little Child each time a wanderer would leave his home. For he must learn that what he would protect is but this Child, Who comes defenseless and Who is protected by defenselessness. Go home with Him from time to time today. You are as much an alien here as He. (W-182.10:1-4)

Take time today to lay aside your shield which profits nothing, and lay down the spear and sword you raised against an enemy without existence. (W-182.11:1)

How Will I Know What Words to Speak?

> "Take no thought how or what ye shall speak: for it shall be given you in that same hour what ye shall speak. For it is not ye that speak, but the Spirit of your Father which speaketh in you." (Matthew 10:19-20)

You can do much on behalf of your own healing and that of others if, in a situation calling for help, you think of it this way:

I am here only to be truly helpful.
I am here to represent Him Who sent me.
I do not have to worry about what to say or what to do,
because He Who sent me will direct me.
I am content to be wherever He wishes, knowing He goes there with me.
I will be healed as I let Him teach me to heal. (T-2.V.A.18:1-6)

> "They are of those that rebel against the light; they know not the ways thereof, nor abide in the paths thereof." (Job 24:13)

> "Show me thy ways, O LORD; teach me thy paths." (Psalms 25:4)

> "Trust in the LORD with all thine heart; and lean not unto thine own understanding. In all thy ways acknowledge him, and he shall direct thy paths." (Proverbs 3:5-6)

Whenever you are in doubt what you should do, think of His Presence in you, and tell yourself this, and only this:

He leadeth me and knows the way, which I know not.
Yet He will never keep from me what He would have me learn.
And so I trust Him to communicate to me all that He knows for me.

Then let Him teach you quietly how to perceive your guiltlessness, which is already there. (T-14.III.19:1-5)

Is it not He Who knows the way to you? You need not know the way to Him. Your part is simply to allow all obstacles that you have interposed between the Son and God the Father to be quietly removed forever. God will do His part in joyful and immediate response. Ask and receive. But do not make demands, nor point the road to God by which He should appear to you. The way to reach Him is merely to let Him be. For in that way is your reality proclaimed as well. (W-189.8:1-8)

And so today we do not choose the way in which we go to Him. But we do choose to let Him come. And with this choice we rest. And in our quiet hearts and open minds, His Love will blaze its pathway of itself. What has not been denied is surely there, if it be true and can be surely reached. God knows His Son, and knows the way to him. He does not need His Son to show Him how to find His way. Through every opened door His Love shines outward from its home within, and lightens up the world in innocence. (W-189.9:1-8)

Steady our feet, our Father. Let our doubts be quiet and our holy minds be still, and speak to us. We have no words to give to You. We would but listen to Your Word, and make it ours. Lead our practicing as does a father lead a little child along a way he does not understand. Yet does he follow, sure that he is safe because his father leads the way for him. (W-rV.in.2:1-6)

So do we bring our practicing to You. And if we stumble, You will raise us up. If we forget the way, we count upon Your sure remembering. We wander off, but You will not forget to call us back. Quicken our footsteps now, that we may walk more certainly and quickly unto You. And we accept the Word You offer us to unify our practicing, as we review the thoughts that You have given us. (W-rV.in.3:1-6)

Speak on Trust

"What time I am afraid, I will trust in thee. In God I will praise his word, in God I have put my trust; I will not fear what flesh can do unto me." (Psalms 56:3-4)

"The God of my rock; in him will I trust: he is my shield, and the horn of my salvation, my high tower, and my refuge, my saviour; thou savest me from violence." (2 Samuel 22:3)

"And they that know thy name will put their trust in thee: for thou, LORD, hast not forsaken them that seek thee." (Psalms 9:10)

"How excellent is thy lovingkindness, O God! therefore the children of men put their trust under the shadow of thy wings." (Psalms 36:7)

"Blessed is that man that maketh the LORD his trust, and respecteth not the proud, nor such as turn aside to lies." (Psalms 40:4)

"Trust in him at all times; ye people, pour out your heart before him: God is a refuge for us." (Psalms 62:8)

"But it is good for me to draw near to God: I have put my trust in the Lord GOD, that I may declare all thy works." (Psalms 73:28)

"And such trust have we through Christ to God-ward." (2 Corinthians 3:4)

Trust

This is the foundation on which their ability to fulfill their function rests. Perception is the result of learning. In fact, perception *is* learning, because cause and effect are never separated. The teachers of God have trust in the world, because they have learned it is not governed by the laws the world made up. It is governed by a power that is *in* them but not *of* them. It is this power that keeps all things safe. It is through this power that the teachers of God look on a forgiven world. (M-4.I.1:1-7)

When this power has once been experienced, it is impossible to trust one's own petty strength again. Who would attempt to fly with the tiny wings of a sparrow when the mighty power of an eagle has been given him? And who would place his faith in the shabby offerings of the ego when the gifts of God are laid before him? (M-4.I.2:1-3)

Development of Trust

First, they must go through what might be called "a period of undoing." This need not be painful, but it usually is so experienced. It seems as if things are being taken away, and it is rarely understood initially that their lack of value is merely being recognized. How can lack of value be perceived unless the perceiver is in a position where he must see things in a different light? He is not yet at a point at which he can make the shift entirely internally. And so the plan will sometimes call for changes in what seem to be external circumstances. These changes are always helpful. When the teacher of God has learned that much, he goes on to the second stage. (M-4.I.A.3:1-8)

Next, the teacher of God must go through "a period of sorting out." This is always somewhat difficult because, having learned that the changes in his life are always helpful, he must now decide all things on the basis of whether they increase the helpfulness or hamper it. He will find that many, if not most of the things he valued before will merely hinder his ability to transfer what he has learned to new situations as they arise. Because he has valued what is really valueless, he will not generalize the lesson for fear of loss and sacrifice. It takes great learning to understand that all things, events, encounters and circumstances are helpful. It is only to the extent to which they are helpful that any degree of reality should be accorded them in this world of illusion. The word "value" can apply to nothing else. (M-4.I.4:1-7)

The third stage through which the teacher of God must go can be called "a period of relinquishment." If this is interpreted as giving up the desirable, it will engender enormous conflict. Few teachers of God escape this distress entirely. There is, however, no point in sorting out the valuable from the valueless unless the next obvious step is taken. Therefore, the period of overlap is apt to be one in which the teacher of God feels called upon to sacrifice his own best interests on behalf of truth. He has not realized as yet how wholly impossible such a demand would be. He can learn this only as he actually does give up the valueless. Through this, he learns that where he anticipated grief, he finds a happy lightheartedness instead; where he thought something was asked of him, he finds a gift bestowed on him. (M-4.I.5:1-8)

Now comes "a period of settling down." This is a quiet time, in which the teacher of God rests a while in reasonable peace. Now he consolidates his learning. Now he begins to see the transfer value of what he has learned. Its potential is literally staggering, and the teacher of God is now at the point in his progress at which he sees in it his whole way out. "Give up what you do not want, and keep what you do." How simple is the obvious! And how easy to do! The teacher of God needs this period of respite. He has not yet come as far as he thinks. Yet when he is ready to go on, he goes with mighty companions beside him. Now he rests a while, and gathers them before going on. He will not go on from here alone. (M-4.I.6:1-13)

The next stage is indeed "a period of unsettling." Now must the teacher of God understand that he did not really know what was valuable and what was valueless. All that he really learned so far was that he did not want the valueless, and that he did want the valuable. Yet his own sorting out was meaningless in teaching him the difference. The idea of sacrifice, so central to his own thought system, had made it impossible for him to judge. He thought he learned willingness, but now he sees that he does not know what the willingness is for. And now he must attain a state that may remain impossible to reach for a long, long time. He must learn to lay all judgment aside, and ask only what he really wants in every circumstance. Were not each step in this direction so heavily reinforced, it would be hard indeed! (M-4.I.7:1-9)

And finally, there is "a period of achievement." It is here that learning is consolidated. Now what was seen as merely shadows before become solid gains, to be counted on in all "emergencies" as well as tranquil times. Indeed, the tranquility is their result; the outcome of honest learning, consistency of thought and full transfer. This is the stage of real peace, for here is Heaven's state fully reflected. From here, the way to Heaven is open and easy. In fact, it is here. Who would "go" anywhere, if peace of mind is already complete? And who would seek to change tranquility for something more desirable? What could be more desirable than this? (M-4.I.8:1-10)

What If I Cannot Do What You Ask?

> "Then came the disciples to Jesus apart, and said, Why could not we cast him out? And Jesus said unto them, Because of your unbelief: for verily I say unto you, If ye have faith as a grain of mustard seed, ye shall say unto this mountain, Remove hence to yonder place; and it shall remove; and nothing shall be impossible unto you." (Matthew 17:19-20)

You can do anything I ask. I have asked you to perform miracles, and have made it clear that miracles are natural, corrective, healing and universal. There is nothing they cannot do, but they cannot be performed in the spirit of doubt or fear. When you are afraid of anything, you are acknowledging its power to hurt you. Remember that where your heart is, there is your treasure also. You believe in what you value. If you are afraid, you are valuing wrongly. Your understanding will then inevitably value wrongly, and by endowing all thoughts with equal power will inevitably destroy peace. That is why the Bible speaks of "the peace of God which passeth understanding." This peace is totally incapable of being shaken by errors of any kind. It denies the ability of anything not of God to affect you. This is the proper use of denial. It is not used to hide anything, but to correct error. It brings all error into the light, and since error and darkness are the same, it corrects error automatically. (T-2.II.1:1-14)

> "Hast thou faith? have it to thyself before God. Happy is he that condemneth not himself in that thing which he alloweth." (Romans 14:22)

See no one, then, as guilty, and you will affirm the truth of guiltlessness unto yourself. In every condemnation that you offer the Son of God lies the conviction of your own guilt. If you would have the Holy Spirit make you free of it, accept His offer of Atonement for all your brothers. For so you learn that it is true for you. Remember always that it is impossible to condemn the Son of God in part. Those whom you see as guilty become the witnesses to guilt in you, and you will see it there, for it *is* there until it is undone. Guilt is always in your mind, which has condemned itself. Project it not, for while you do, it cannot be undone. With everyone whom you release from guilt great is the joy in Heaven, where the witnesses to your fatherhood rejoice. (T-13.IX.6:1-9)

Blessed Son of a wholly blessing Father, joy was created for you. Who can condemn whom God has blessed? There is nothing in the Mind of God that does not share His shining innocence. Creation is the natural extension of perfect purity. (T-14.V.3:1-4)

To have faith is to heal. It is the sign that you have accepted the Atonement for yourself, and would therefore share it. By faith, you offer the gift of freedom from the past, which you received. You do not use anything your brother has done before to condemn him now. You freely choose to overlook his errors, looking past all barriers between yourself and him, and seeing them as one. (T-19.I.9:1-5)

> "Jesus beheld them, and said unto them, With men this is impossible; but with God all things are possible." (Matthew 19:26)

God's Son *is* saved. Bring only this awareness to the Sonship, and you will have a part in the redemption as valuable as mine. For your part must be like mine if you learn it of me. If you believe that yours is limited, you are limiting mine. There is no order of difficulty in miracles because all of God's Sons are of equal value, and their equality is their oneness. The whole power of God is in every part of Him, and nothing contradictory to His Will is either great or small. What does not exist has no size and no measure. To God all things are possible. And to Christ it is given to be like the Father. (T-11.VI.10:1-9)

> "A Psalm of David. The LORD is my shepherd; I shall not want. He maketh me to lie down in green pastures: he leadeth me beside the still waters. He restoreth my soul: he leadeth me in the paths of righteousness for his name's sake. Yea, though I walk through the valley of the shadow of death, I will fear no evil: for thou art with me; thy rod and thy staff they comfort me. Thou preparest a table before me in the presence of mine enemies: thou anointest my head with oil; my cup runneth over. Surely goodness and mercy shall follow me all the days of my life: and I will dwell in the house of the LORD for ever." (Psalms 23:1-6)

When you have accepted the Atonement for yourself, you will realize there is no guilt in God's Son. And only as you look upon him as guiltless can you understand his oneness. For the idea of guilt brings a belief in condemnation of one by another, projecting separation in place of unity. You can condemn only yourself, and by so doing you cannot know that you are God's Son. You have denied the condition of his being, which is his perfect blamelessness. Out of love he was created, and in love he abides. Goodness and mercy have always followed him, for he has always extended the Love of his Father. (T-13.I.6:1-7)

> "He saith unto them, It is I; be not afraid." (John 6:20)

What is healing but the removal of all that stands in the way of knowledge? And how else can one dispel illusions except by looking at them directly, without protecting them? Be not afraid, therefore, for what you will be looking at is the source of fear, and you are beginning to learn that fear is not real. You are also learning that its effects can be dispelled merely by denying their reality. The next step is obviously to recognize that what has no effects does not exist. Laws do not operate in a vacuum, and what leads to nothing has not happened. If reality is recognized by its extension, what leads to nothing could not be real. Do not be afraid, then, to look upon fear, for it cannot be seen. Clarity undoes confusion by definition, and to look upon darkness through light must dispel it. (T-11.V.2:1-9)

> "Be strong and of a good courage, fear not, nor be afraid of them: for the LORD thy God, he it is that doth go with thee; he will not fail thee, nor forsake thee." (Deuteronomy 31:6)

Forget not that the motivation for this course is the attainment and the keeping of the state of peace. Given this state the mind is quiet, and the condition in which God is remembered is attained. It is not necessary to tell Him what to do. He will not fail. Where He can enter, there He is already. And can it be He cannot enter where He wills to be? Peace will be yours *because* it is His Will. (T-24.in.1:1-7)

> "For thou wilt not leave my soul in hell; neither wilt thou suffer thine Holy One to see corruption. Thou wilt show me the path of life: in thy presence is fullness of joy; at thy right hand there are pleasures for evermore." (Psalms 16:10-11)

Have faith in only this one thing, and it will be sufficient: God wills you be in Heaven, and nothing can keep you from it, or it from you. Your wildest misperceptions, your weird imaginings, your blackest nightmares all mean nothing. They will not prevail against the peace God wills for you. The Holy Spirit will restore your sanity because insanity is not the Will of God. If that suffices Him, it is enough for you. You will not keep what God would have removed, because it breaks communication with you with whom He would communicate. His Voice *will* be heard. (T-13.XI.7:1-7)

Speak on Your Appearance on the Road to Emmaus

"Lo, he goeth by me, and I see him not: he passeth on also, but I perceive him not." (Job 9:11)

"And, behold, two of them went that same day to a village called Emmaus, which was from Jerusalem about threescore furlongs. And they talked together of all these things which had happened. And it came to pass, that, while they communed together and reasoned, Jesus himself drew near, and went with them. But their eyes were holden that they should not know him.

And he said unto them, What manner of communications are these that ye have one to another, as ye walk, and are sad? And the one of them, whose name was Cleopas, answering said unto him, Art thou only a stranger in Jerusalem, and hast not known the things which are come to pass there in these days?

And he said unto them, What things? And they said unto him, Concerning Jesus of Nazareth, which was a prophet mighty in deed and word before God and all the people: And how the chief priests and our rulers delivered him to be condemned to death, and have crucified him. But we trusted that it had been he which should have redeemed Israel: and beside all this, to day is the third day since these things were done. Yea, and certain women also of our company made us astonished, which were early at the sepulchre; And when they found not his body, they came, saying, that they had also seen a vision of angels, which said that he was alive. And certain of them which were with us went to the sepulchre, and found it even so as the women had said: but him they saw not.

Then he said unto them, O fools, and slow of heart to believe all that the prophets have spoken: Ought not Christ to have suffered these things, and to enter into his glory? And beginning at Moses and all the prophets, he expounded unto them in all the scriptures the things concerning himself.

> And they drew nigh unto the village, whither they went: and he made as though he would have gone further. But they constrained him, saying, Abide with us: for it is toward evening, and the day is far spent. And he went in to tarry with them. And it came to pass, as he sat at meat with them, he took bread, and blessed it, and brake, and gave to them. And their eyes were opened, and they knew him; and he vanished out of their sight." (Luke 24:13-31)

If you knew Who walks beside you on the way that you have chosen, fear would be impossible. You do not know because the journey into darkness has been long and cruel, and you have gone deep into it. A little flicker of your eyelids, closed so long, has not yet been sufficient to give you confidence in yourself, so long despised. You go toward love still hating it, and terribly afraid of its judgment upon you. And you do not realize that you are not afraid of love, but only of what you have made of it. You are advancing to love's meaning, and away from all illusions in which you have surrounded it. When you retreat to the illusion your fear increases, for there is little doubt that what you think it means *is* fearful. Yet what is that to us who travel surely and very swiftly away from fear? (T-18.III.3:2-9)

Think of the loveliness that you will see, who walk with Him! And think how beautiful will you and your brother look to the other! How happy you will be to be together, after such a long and lonely journey where you walked alone. The gates of Heaven, open now for you, will you now open to the sorrowful. And none who looks upon the Christ in you but will rejoice. How beautiful the sight you saw beyond the veil, which you will bring to light the tired eyes of those as weary now as once you were. How thankful will they be to see you come among them, offering Christ's forgiveness to dispel their faith in sin. (T-22.IV.4:1-7)

> "Jesus saith unto her, Touch me not; for I am not yet ascended to my Father: but go to my brethren, and say unto them, I ascend unto my Father, and your Father; and to my God, and your God." (John 20:17)

> "Jesus saith unto him, Thomas, because thou hast seen me, thou hast believed: blessed are they that have not seen, and yet have believed." (John 20:29)

It is impossible not to believe what you see, but it is equally impossible to see what you do not believe. Perceptions are built up on the basis of experience, and experience leads to beliefs. It is not until beliefs are fixed that perceptions stabilize. In effect, then, what you believe you *do* see. That is what I meant when I said, "Blessed are ye who have not seen and still believe," for those who believe in the resurrection will see it. The resurrection is the complete triumph of Christ over the ego, not by attack but by transcendence. For Christ does rise above the ego and all its works, and ascends to the Father and His Kingdom. (T-11.VI.1:1-7)

Resurrection must compel your allegiance gladly, because it is the symbol of joy. Its whole compelling power lies in the fact that it represents what you want to be. The freedom to leave behind everything that hurts you and humbles you and frightens you cannot be thrust upon you, but it can be offered you through the grace of God. And you can accept it by His grace, for God is gracious to His Son, accepting him without question as His Own. Who, then, is *your* own? The Father has given you all that is His, and He Himself is yours with them. Guard them in their resurrection, for otherwise you will not awake in God, safely surrounded by what is yours forever. (T-11.VI.6:1-7)

You will awaken to your own call, for the Call to awake is within you. If I live in you, you are awake. Yet you must see the works I do through you, or you will not perceive that I have done them unto you. Do not set limits on what you believe I can do through you, or you will not accept what I can do *for* you. Yet it is done already, and unless you give all that you have received you will not know that your redeemer liveth, and that you have awakened with him. Redemption is recognized only by sharing it. (T-11.VI.9:1-6)

> "And I will pray the Father, and he shall give you another Comforter, that he may abide with you for ever; Even the Spirit of truth; whom the world cannot receive, because it seeth him not, neither knoweth him: but ye know him; for he dwelleth with you, and shall be in you." (John 14:16-17)

The Holy Spirit is the only part of the Holy Trinity that has a symbolic function. He is referred to as the Healer, the Comforter and the Guide. He is also described as something "separate," apart from the Father and from the Son. I myself said, "If I go I will send you another Comforter and he will abide with you." His symbolic function makes the Holy Spirit difficult to understand, because symbolism is open to different interpretations. As a man and also one of God's creations, my right thinking, which came from the Holy Spirit or the Universal Inspiration, taught me first and foremost that this Inspiration is for all. I could not have It myself without knowing this. The word "know" is proper in this context, because the Holy Spirit is so close to knowledge that He calls it forth; or better, allows it to come. I have spoken before of the higher or "true" perception, which is so near to truth that God Himself can flow across the little gap. Knowledge is always ready to flow everywhere, but it cannot oppose. Therefore you can obstruct it, although you can never lose it. (T-5.I.4:1-11)

The Holy Spirit calls you both to remember and to forget. You have chosen to be in a state of opposition in which opposites are possible. As a result, there are choices you must make. In the holy state the will is free, so that its creative power is unlimited and choice is meaningless. Freedom to choose is the same power as freedom to create, but its application is different. Choosing depends on a split mind. The Holy Spirit is one way of choosing. God did not leave His children comfortless, even though they chose to leave Him. The voice they put in their minds was not the Voice for His Will, for which the Holy Spirit speaks. (T-5.II.6:1-9)

The Voice of the Holy Spirit does not command, because It is incapable of arrogance. It does not demand, because It does not seek control. It does not overcome, because It does not attack. It merely reminds. It is compelling only because of what It reminds you *of.* It brings to your mind the other way, remaining quiet even in the midst of the turmoil you may make. The Voice for God is always quiet, because It speaks of peace. Peace is stronger than war because it heals. War is division, not increase. No one gains from strife. What profiteth it a man if he gain the whole world and lose his own soul? If you listen to the wrong voice you *have* lost sight of your soul. You cannot lose it, but you can not know it. It is therefore "lost" to you until you choose right. (T-5.II.7:1-14)

The Holy Spirit is your Guide in choosing. He is in the part of your mind that always speaks for the right choice, because He speaks for God. He is your remaining communication with God, which you can interrupt but cannot destroy. The Holy Spirit is the way in which God's Will is done on earth as it is in Heaven. Both Heaven and earth are in you, because the call of both is in your mind. The Voice for God comes from your own altars to Him. These altars are not things; they are devotions. Yet you have other devotions now. Your divided devotion has given you the two voices, and you must choose at which altar you want to serve. The call you answer now is an evaluation because it is a decision. The decision is very simple. It is made on the basis of which call is worth more to you. (T-5.II.8:1-12)

> "Who only hath immortality, dwelling in the light which no man can approach unto; whom no man hath seen, nor can see: to whom be honour and power everlasting. Amen." (1 Timothy 6:16)

> "I will instruct thee and teach thee in the way which thou shalt go: I will guide thee with mine eye." (Psalms 32:8)

The single vision which the Holy Spirit offers you will bring this oneness to your mind with clarity and brightness so intense you could not wish, for all the world, not to accept what God would have you have. Behold your will, accepting it as His, with all His Love as yours. All honor to you through Him, and through Him unto God. (T-14.VII.7:7-9)

> "Let your conversation be without covetousness; and be content with such things as ye have: for he hath said, I will never leave thee, nor forsake thee." (Hebrews 13:5)

I will never leave you or forsake you, because to forsake you would be to forsake myself and God Who created me. You forsake yourself and God if you forsake any of your brothers. You must learn to see them as they are, and understand they belong to God as you do. How could you treat your brother better than by rendering unto God the things that are God's? (T-5.IV.6:5-8)

> "Lord, now lettest thou thy servant depart in peace, according to thy word." (Luke 2:29)

You can indeed depart in peace because I have loved you as I loved myself. You go with my blessing and for my blessing. Hold it and share it, that it may always be ours. I place the peace of God in your heart and in your hands, to hold and share. The heart is pure to hold it, and the hands are strong to give it. We cannot lose. My judgment is as strong as the wisdom of God, in Whose Heart and Hands we have our being. His quiet children are His blessed Sons. The Thoughts of God are with you. (T-5.IV.8:7-15)

> "Peace I leave with you, my peace I give unto you: not as the world giveth, give I unto you. Let not your heart be troubled, neither let it be afraid." (John 14:27)

When I said, "My peace I give unto you," I meant it. Peace comes from God through me to you. It is for you although you may not ask for it. (T-10.III.6:6-8)

Peace, then, be unto everyone who becomes a teacher of peace. For peace is the acknowledgment of perfect purity, from which no one is excluded. Within its holy circle is everyone whom God created as His Son. Joy is its unifying attribute, with no one left outside to suffer guilt alone. The power of God draws everyone to its safe embrace of love and union. Stand quietly within this circle, and attract all tortured minds to join with you in the safety of its peace and holiness. Abide with me within it, as a teacher of Atonement, not of guilt. (T-14.V.8:1-7)

Peace be to you to whom is healing offered. And you will learn that peace is given you when you accept the healing for yourself. (T-27.V.11:1-2)

> "Finally, brethren, whatsoever things are true, whatsoever things are honest, whatsoever things are just, whatsoever things are pure, whatsoever things are lovely, whatsoever things are of good report; if there be any virtue, and if there be any praise, think on these things." (Philippians 4:8)

> "Create in me a clean heart, O God; and renew a right spirit within me." (Psalms 51:10)

> "These words spake Jesus, and lifted up his eyes to heaven, and said, Father, the hour is come; glorify thy Son, that thy Son also may glorify thee: As thou hast given him power over all flesh, that he should give eternal life to as many as thou hast given him. And this is life eternal, that they might know thee the only true God, and Jesus Christ, whom thou hast sent. I have glorified thee on the earth: I have finished the work which thou gavest me to do.

And now, O Father, glorify thou me with thine own self with the glory which I had with thee before the world was. I have manifested thy name unto the men which thou gavest me out of the world: thine they were, and thou gavest them me; and they have kept thy word. Now they have known that all things whatsoever thou hast given me are of thee. For I have given unto them the words which thou gavest me; and they have received [them], and have known surely that I came out from thee, and they have believed that thou didst send me.

I pray for them: I pray not for the world, but for them which thou hast given me; for they are thine. And all mine are thine, and thine are mine; and I am glorified in them. And now I am no more in the world, but these are in the world, and I come to thee. Holy Father, keep through thine own name those whom thou hast given me, that they may be one, as we are." (John 17:1-11)

"These things have I spoken unto you, that my joy might remain in you, and that your joy might be full." (John 15:11)

"And, lo, I am with you always, even unto the end of the world. Amen." (Matthew 28:20)

The Holy Spirit teaches one lesson, and applies it to all individuals in all situations. Being conflict-free, He maximizes all efforts and all results. By teaching the power of the Kingdom of God Himself, He teaches you that all power is yours. Its application does not matter. It is always maximal. Your vigilance does not establish it as yours, but it does enable you to use it always and in all ways. When I said "I am with you always," I meant it literally. I am not absent to anyone in any situation. Because I am always with you, *you* are the way, the truth and the life. You did not make this power, any more than I did. It was created to be shared, and therefore cannot be meaningfully perceived as belonging to anyone at the expense of another. (T-7.III.1:1-11)

This course is a beginning, not an end. Your Friend goes with you. You are not alone. No one who calls on Him can call in vain. Whatever troubles you, be certain that He has the answer, and will gladly give it to you, if you simply turn to Him and ask it of Him. He will not withhold all answers that you need for anything that seems to trouble you. He knows the way to solve all problems, and resolve all doubts. His certainty is yours. You need but ask it of Him, and it will be given you. (W-Ep.1:1-9)

You are as certain of arriving home as is the pathway of the sun laid down before it rises, after it has set, and in the half-lit hours in between. Indeed, your pathway is more certain still. For it can not be possible to change the course of those whom God has called to Him. Therefore obey your will, and follow Him Whom you accepted as your voice, to speak of what you really want and really need. His is the Voice for God and also yours. And thus He speaks of freedom and of truth. (W-Ep.2:1-6)

Henceforth, hear but the Voice for God and for your Self when you retire from the world, to seek reality instead. He will direct your efforts, telling you exactly what to do, how to direct your mind, and when to come to Him in silence, asking for His sure direction and His certain Word. His is the Word that God has given you. His is the Word you chose to be your own. (W-Ep.3:2-5)

And now I place you in His hands, to be His faithful follower, with Him as Guide through every difficulty and all pain that you may think is real. Nor will He give you pleasures that will pass away, for He gives only the eternal and the good. Let Him prepare you further. He has earned your trust by speaking daily to you of your Father and your brother and your Self. He will continue. Now you walk with Him, as certain as is He of where you go; as sure as He of how you should proceed; as confident as He is of the goal, and of your safe arrival in the end. (W-Ep.4:1-6)

The end is certain, and the means as well. To this we say "Amen." You will be told exactly what God wills for you each time there is a choice to make. And He will speak for God and for your Self, thus making sure that hell will claim you not, and that each choice you make brings Heaven nearer to your reach. And so we walk with Him from this time on, and turn to Him for guidance and for peace and sure direction. Joy attends our way. For we go homeward to an open door which God has held unclosed to welcome us. (W-Ep.5:1-7)

We trust our ways to Him and say "Amen." In peace we will continue in His way, and trust all things to Him. In confidence we wait His answers, as we ask His Will in everything we do. He loves God's Son as we would love him. And He teaches us how to behold him through His eyes, and love him as He does. You do not walk alone. God's angels hover near and all about. His Love surrounds you, and of this be sure; that I will never leave you comfortless. (W-Ep.6:1-8)

Now is the first
and only moment
of a life of rest and Peace!

David Hoffmeister

Mystic David Hoffmeister is a living demonstration that peace is possible. His gentle demeanor and articulate, non-compromising expression are a gift to all. He is known for his practical application of the non-dual teachings necessary to experience a consistently peaceful state of mind. The purity of the message he shares points directly to the Source. Over the past thirty years, David has traveled to forty-one countries across six continents to extend the message that Truth is available for everyone, now.

David's message speaks to all people, regardless of whether their background is religious, spiritual, or scientific. He is as comfortable delving into the metaphysics of modern-day movies as he is in pointing to the underlying meaning of the scriptures in the Bible.

David's own journey involved the study of many pathways, culminating in a deeply committed practical application of *A Course in Miracles,* of which he is a world-renowned teacher. His teachings have been translated into twelve languages, and taken into the hearts and minds of millions through the intimate style of his books, audios, and videos.

The Mystical Experience ends the world of duality and conflict forever and is one of clarity, great joy, deep peace and tranquility. The Experience is not of this world, but radiates from within. It is not a concept; it comes into awareness when all concepts have been laid by. Forgiveness is the last concept. "To Have, Give All to All." (T-6.V.A)

Also by David Hoffmeister

The Answer
Going Deeper
Only One Mind
Healing in Mind
A Glimpse of Grace
Pearls from the Mind Awake
Purpose Is the Only Choice
Unwind Your Mind Back to God
Awakening through *A Course in Miracles*
Movie Watcher's Guide to Enlightenment
Quantum Forgiveness: Physics, Meet Jesus

Enjoy David's writings in print, eBook and audiobook formats. Select materials have been translated into Chinese, Danish, Dutch, Finnish, French, Hungarian, Japanese, Norwegian, Portuguese, Spanish and Swedish.

Online Resources

Visit **DavidHoffmeister.com** to learn more about David and his teachings. Enjoy a wealth of online materials for awakening at the **ACIM.biz** website. Visit **LivingMiracles.org** for information about our inspired communities, online events, and retreats around the world.